Finding Our Way with the Magi

A Daily Guide Through the Season of Advent

John Michael Helms

Published in the United States by FaithLab, Macon GA.
www.thefaithlab.com

ISBN 978-0-9839863-0-0

Also by
John Michael Helms

Finding Our Way: An Introspective Journey
Through the Labyrinth of Life

Hoping Liberia:
Stories of Civil War from
Africa's First Republic

What Others Say

Michael Helms clears away the layers of wrappings, ribbons, and assorted commercial glitz, so that once again we can gaze upon the Christ Child. These delightful, often touching reflections usher us gracefully through the Advent season.

Dr. Jim Barnette
Professor, Samford University
Teaching Pastor
Brookwood Baptist Church
Birmingham, Alabama

Finding Our Way with the Magi offers a unique opportunity for those who long for a meaningful spiritual discipline during the season of Advent. The imposed busyness around us, and the often pain-filled associations of the holidays often distract us, if not prevent us altogether from encountering God, even in this holiest of seasons. With the narrative grace of a gifted pastor, Michael Helms offers meaningful devotional engagement along with thoughtful direction for actually living through the Advent season with purpose and intention. The inclusion of helpful and accessible appendices offers even deeper engagement. Even for the casual reader who longs, as we all do, to put aside the trappings of our cultural Christmas celebration and remember, in deep and life-transforming ways, the holy promise of God With Us.

Rev. Dr. Amy Butler
Senior Pastor
Calvary Baptist Church
Washington, DC

Michael Helms' *Finding Our Way with the Magi: A Daily Guide Through the Season of Advent* is a Christ-centered GPS that will navigate your family through the Advent season with a gentleness and grace that foster the peace and hope so often absent in the daily bustle of life.

The daily reflections are memorable and personal, offering families a time to focus on the true meaning of the season. Helms' stories will cause you to pause for personal reflection and recollection, while "Advent Actions" will nudge you to put your faith into action in practical ways. In addition, the daily prayer offers guidance for a few moments of focused quietness in communicating with the Giver of the Advent season.

This Advent season, find your way with the Magi by making this volume a part of your family's daily life.

Dr. Bruce Gourley
Executive Director
Baptist History & Heritage Society
www.baptisthistory.org

Michael Helms provides an exceptional and straightforward guide that connects Christmas to Christ especially in our world that connects Christmas to commercialization. Helms' *Finding Our Way with the Magi* is a reflective Advent reading that points the reader to the essence of the Christmas story.

Dr. Olu Q. Menjay
Vice President, Baptist World Alliance (2010-2015)
Chief Administrative Officer/Principal—Ricks Institute, Liberia
www.ricksonline.org

Dedication

Gold: I think of my wife Tina and of the rings we exchanged in 1984 that represent our love for one another. It only grows deeper with the passing of time.

Frankincense: I think of my mother Lenora and her calming, restorative, warming, medicinal qualities she brings to our family.

Myrrh: I think of my mother-in-law Minnie. I realize this resin was used for embalming. All mother-in-law jokes aside, Minnie has encased my marriage to Tina with a sweetness that I hope our sons will one day be lucky enough to have in a mother-in-law.

Acknowledgments

The acknowledgment page is the author's chance to mention anybody and everybody that's had something to do with the book's publication.

A lot of people skip this page, so since you are reading it, I'd like to begin by thanking you. Yes, you! Thank you for buying this book and taking this Advent journey. I commend you for this intentional step, and I pray that God will use this book to bless your Advent season and your Christian journey.

My Christian journey has taken me back to North Georgia. I now pastor First Baptist Church of Jefferson, Georgia, where our interest in missions, both local and international, is strong and our love for worship is deep. I am blessed to pastor this wonderful group of people and to do life with them.

However, this book developed mostly through my ministry in my previous pastorate at Trinity Baptist Church in Moultrie, Georgia, where I pastored for thirteen years. Through my weekly articles with the *Moultrie Observer* I found a discipline for writing. I will always be thankful to Dwain Walden for giving me that opportunity.

Andrea Savage, a member of Trinity Baptist, has been my trusted proofreader through the years. She, along with Dr. Diana Young, a member of First Baptist Church of Jefferson, has been a tremendous help on this project, as well as others I have done.

I am thankful to those who took time out of their very busy schedules to read this book and give you their recommendation. These are people I highly respect and greatly value as endorsers of my book.

I am also grateful to Dr. Jim Dant and Dr. David Cassady for partnering with me in publishing this book and its companion book to follow on Lent.

Finally, thanks to all those people in my past who have made the season of Advent: a season of wonder, a season of expectation, a season of joy, a season of memories, a season of love, and a season to pause and reflect on the miracle of the birth of the Christ Child. I could never name all of you, but you are a part of me. Whether you are named in this book or not, in some way you are a part of this book. In some way you are a part of every Advent I live.

John Michael Helms
March 2011

Table of Contents

Journeying with the Magi

Introduction

In America, as soon as merchants take Halloween merchandise from the shelves, they begin putting up the first signs of Christmas, nearly two full months before Christmas Day. You can't fault them for getting such an early start. Sales in October, November, and December can account for as much as half of their yearly sales.

By and large, Americans have bought into the idea that Christmas is about giving and receiving gifts. Should we give credit or blame to the astrologers who followed the star to the place where Jesus was born for starting this Christmas tradition? After all, they came bearing gifts of gold, frankincense, and myrrh on that first Christmas.

While gift giving is a joyous practice, some have made this the central part of the holiday season. We can't find the baby wrapped in swaddling clothes because He is buried under a mountain of wrapping paper, bows, and ribbons that lie beneath hundreds of shining lights, which we hang on our trees and in our homes.

In the midst of all the gift giving, decorating, and other Christmas festivities, if we do not intentionally focus on our relationship with Jesus during the days leading up to Christmas, we will fail to allow the One whom the season is all about to cast any light on our lives. Consequently, darkness will crowd out any real joy, peace, love, and hope that we might give or receive. Most of us will hang lights to decorate during the holidays, but more importantly, we need a Light to shine in the darkness of our lives to help us find our way through Advent.

Unfortunately, too many people move through these days before Christmas, called Advent, to Christmas Day and beyond, and find that the season feels as artificial as the trees they place in their homes. Like clowns, many people paint on their smiles. Many go from party to party looking for an escape to numb their feelings of loneliness and emptiness. They pretend to be happy right through New Year's Day.

Finally, when the holidays are over, they peel off their fake smiles and awake to the realities of huge credit card debt, empty houses, trees they have no desire to take down, but no desire to leave up, and the beginning of what feels like depression. Some even think they hate the holidays and are grateful for one thing—that the holidays come only once a year. Isn't there something we can do to prevent such a thing from happening?

Even if the above doesn't describe you totally, many of you have experienced enough of the holiday blues to know that the season brings its own set of challenges in the midst of its promised good cheer.

We are all on a journey, just like Joseph and Mary so long ago. We all have plans, but our plans get interrupted; they can change in an instant, for good or bad. The couple didn't plan on making a trip to Bethlehem in the ninth month of Mary's pregnancy. Thanks to Caesar Augustus, Joseph had no choice but to travel back to his hometown to be counted for tax purposes. They didn't plan on there being no room in the inn. With no way to call ahead for reservations, there was no way to plan for Mary to have a comfortable place to bed, as her labor pains increased, and the intervals between labor pains shortened.

We all know what it's like for plans to suddenly change. All it takes is for one of our kids to fall down the steps and break a tooth, and our morning is spent at the dentist's office, instead of visiting Santa at the mall. All it takes is for a college daughter to come home for the holidays without an understanding that there are still curfews at home that must be obeyed. Otherwise, the peace of a holiday evening is filled with worry and anxiety as we wait and wait, far past midnight, for her to arrive home. All it takes is for an ex-spouse to change the day he or she wants the children to visit or for the boss to change his or her mind about the time we can have off from our job.

Life is full of changes we didn't plan. The Christmas bonus is cut. The store that promised the special gift you had ordered for your child called and said it wasn't coming after all. The spouse who promised he or she wouldn't drink during the holidays is not only drinking, but is drinking more than usual. The receptionist called from the doctor's office and said the biopsy was positive, and they need to schedule you for a follow-up appointment to discuss the next step. Plans get changed, and life can be turned upside down in a heartbeat. This Advent, at some point, your plans will get changed, too. It may not be life changing, but one never knows.

Of course, plans can also change for the better. We don't tend to think a lot about these times because we absorb them into life like a hummingbird joyfully sucking sugar water from a feeder. Most of us don't stop often enough to flag these God-given times and give thanks: an unexpected Christmas bonus, friends who call and offer to keep your children so that you and your spouse can enjoy a night together, a child or grandchild who hops in your lap and shows love to you without any coercion on your part. It's those blind-sided, "I had no choice in the matter" changes that throw us off track and push us to our knees.

We are all on a journey, so we all need a light to shine in the dark places and in the shadows to illuminate our paths. Many people run their lives like a car, with no lights burning, going eighty miles per hour down a dark road. When they hit something, they say,

"I didn't see it coming." They act surprised.

Others live a more measured, calculated life. Yet not even these people can be prepared for every event of life.

On that first Christmas, those who were living the measured, calculated lives were the Magi. They had studied the stars, and all their indications pointed them toward the birth of a Savior, so they came looking for the Christ Child to worship Him. They came bearing gifts. They weren't caught up in anything materialistic. Their gifts were genuine expressions of adoration. Unlike much of our gift-giving, they weren't looking to receive anything in return other than the satisfaction of worshiping a child their signs indicated would grow to become a world ruler.

The journey was long. In the year 8 BC, Cuneiform tablets from Sippar in Babylonia revealed the foretelling of the rare conjunction of Jupiter and Saturn that would occur the next year, a phenomenon that happens only once in 794 years. To the men of antiquity, this aligning of the planets had a special meaning. The planet Jupiter represented a world ruler while Saturn was considered the star of Palestine. The astrologers saw this as a sign that a world ruler would be born the next year in Palestine. Thus, they showed up in 7 BC in Jerusalem, just down the road from Bethlehem, looking for the birth of this king.[1] (Scholars debate the exact date of Jesus' birth.)

The journey likely took a month, maybe two. That meant it would have taken that long to return. Think of the sacrifices and planning that went into making the long, risky journey, just to worship, just to see this child, just to bring Him and His family gifts.

While we cannot prepare for every situation that has the potential to harm us, we can learn to stop being our own worst enemies. We can identify some of the "fast driving at night with no headlights" kind of living and eliminate those times in our lives. Secondly, we can learn to be intentional with the Light and shine Christ in the areas of our lives where we need to see the path with more clarity.

If we are going to find our way through Advent, we need the intentionality of the astrologers, who journeyed to worship the newborn King. How do we become more like the astrologers, whom we meet in Matthew's gospel, the "Magi" as they are often called?

It's not much of a stretch to imagine that the Magi must have spent many months, perhaps even a year in prayer, planning, and preparation for a trip that would take a couple of months across various terrain in unpredictable weather. Remember, they didn't have a global positioning system. As men of faith, they probably began their trip by asking for God's guidance. If so, they had the best model G.P.S. (God's Positioning System) to help put their plans and preparation into action. We do know that God came to them in a dream, warning them not to return to Herod as they had planned.

We are also in need of God's Positioning System. Advent is filled with planning and preparation of meals, trips, purchasing and exchanging gifts, parties, socials, and visits to see Santa. With all the demands of our time, the One in the center of the manger scene gets pushed further and further out of our picture so that the birthday for Jesus is more of a Christmas mourning than a Christmas morning for Him. He mourns that we've lost Him in the midst of it all.

Advent is a season designed to change that. It is a time of preparation for Christmas Day. Advent means "coming" or "arriving." It's a countdown of sorts to the birthday of Jesus. It's an opportunity to reflect on the coming of Jesus in Bethlehem, the coming of Jesus in our everyday lives, and the promise of Jesus' Second Coming.

When I was a child, my aunt, uncle, and cousins, the Turk family, would visit from South Florida every summer and usually at Thanksgiving. I looked forward with great anticipation to their visits. They brought fruit and hand-me-down clothes. My cousin Steven is a month older than I and was always a jean size and shirt size larger. I always enjoyed secondhand clothes, especially the jeans. I always thought they were better than the store-bought ones. Years later, the jeans stores proved me right. They started selling new jeans that looked like used jeans with the holes already in them.

The day the Turks arrived had to be the longest day of the year for me, longer than Christmas Eve. I sat on my grandparents' front porch and looked in anticipation, hoping every car that came around the curve would be theirs.

For centuries, the people of Israel had waited and longed for God to send the promised Messiah. The prophets had foretold His coming. When Jesus was born, the scripture tells us that Mary and Joseph took Him to the temple in Jerusalem on the eighth day for His circumcision and to make a sacrifice to God. The scripture says:

> *There was a man in Jerusalem called Simeon, who was righteous and devout. He was waiting for the consolation of Israel, and the Holy Spirit was upon him. It had been revealed to him by the Holy Spirit that he would not die before he had seen the Lord's Christ. Moved by the Spirit, he went into the temple courts. When the parents brought in the child Jesus to do for him what the custom of the Law required, Simeon took him in his arms and praised God, saying: 'Sovereign Lord, as you have promised, you now dismiss your servant in peace. For my eyes have seen your salvation, which you have prepared in the sight of all people, a light for revelation to the Gentiles and for glory to your people Israel' (Luke 2:25-32).*

Simeon helps us understand the meaning of Advent. He had been waiting for the consolation of Israel. What does that mean? The word "consolation" in Greek is paraklesis. It comes from the root, parakaleo, which means to "call near, to invite, invoke." In other words, Simeon was not just sitting around the temple as if he had an appointment with the Lord at some unknown date in the future. No. If you had gone to the temple, you would have noticed Simeon.

He was constantly praying, looking intently at every child who came into the temple. Simeon's waiting was active. Most never knew exactly what Simeon was waiting for, but he knew. God gave him a promise, so he remained on alert. He knew any child who came into the temple could be the Promised One—any child. So he waited and waited and waited. We don't know how long. Months? Years perhaps? Every day was filled with expectation, and the promises of hope, peace, joy, and love breaking into the world, in a new way that the world had never seen or known.

How much hope, peace, joy, and love can we call near, invite, or invoke into our lives? We need a little parakaleo ourselves. If we just wait passively for it all to come to us, much of it will pass us by like a ship in the night.

"Worship" is a verb. It is active. It should be no less active than the effort the Magi gave in planning their trip and making the journey to worship the Christ Child, no less active than Simeon waiting for the Christ Child to arrive in the temple.

When we think of worship, we often think of what happens inside a church or when people gather in a small group. While there is movement of one's heart, as one is confronted with sin and the need for change, combined with people moving their voices in praise to God through song and prayers, it is important to remember that this movement must then be put into practice once the worship experience has concluded.

It has been said that we gather for worship, but we scatter for service. Actually, service is part of the way we worship. This is illustrated well in a story of a group of people who had:

...gathered to pray for a family who was going through a

difficult time financially. They were broke, out of work, and the prospects of finding work were slim. As one man was praying fervently, there was a knock at the door. They stopped, opened the door and there stood a sturdy boy. The man said, 'What do you want, boy?' The boy replied, 'Pa couldn't come, so I brought his prayers in the pickup. Just come and help me, please, and we'll bring them in.' Pa's 'prayers' consisted of meat, potatoes, flour, beef, vegetables, apples and jellies. The prayer meeting broke up pretty quickly after that.[2]

This is not to diminish the importance of prayer. It is to emphasize the importance of putting legs to our prayers. The Magi didn't expect the newly born king to come to them. They knew if they were to have the opportunity to worship this newly born king, they had to go find Him.

Now, I realize that Jesus is all about finding us. I know Jesus' story of the lost sheep, how the Good Shepherd leaves the ninety-nine in the fold to go look for the one that is lost. However, that is not to say that we do not have a responsibility to search for Christ during this season of Advent. We should not expect Christmas to come to us. Oh, it might, and if it does, what a gift!

Advent is about calling the season near to us. More than that, it's about inviting a Savior to be near to us, to come to us, to speak to us, to guide our lives, to convict us and forgive us of sin, to show us the path of righteousness, and to bless us, not for our sakes only, but so we in turn can bless others. That may involve taking our prayers to people the way the boy delivered the prayers of his Pa.

If we do not expect Christ to come, if we do not invoke the coming of Christ, if we do not profess that Christ has come or is coming again, the chances are not good that we are going to be very concerned about blessing others.

There is no doubt that America has begun to crumble under her own weight of greed and self-indulgence. We are a country where self-sacrifice is becoming a laughable concept, and every person for himself or herself is the norm. We are the country where the executive often gets the golden parachute while the employee who's worked for the company for twenty-six years gets the shaft. We are becoming a nation of greedy people who care only about self-preservation.

We have allowed greed to become so widespread that our financial institutions are crumbling around us to the point that the foundations of our society have been threatened. While our nation has focused military power on those countries that can attack us from without, the cancers of greed and unethical practices have been growing from within.

Consequently, companies have collapsed, driving down the stock market. Our prisons are running out of room to house inmates. Families are falling apart, and children find pleasure and attention in all the wrong places. The bar for dignity and decency has been lowered so low that we are no longer shocked; we seem to be headed for disaster.

However, there is one thing greater than all the evils of humanity; it is the hope of humanity, the hope that the greatest of evil minds and intentions of evil can be overcome by the hope and love of men and women, boys and girls, who refuse to allow circumstances of hardship and suffering to overwhelm their lives and steal all their joy. The suffering and hardship can be overcome only through the Advent of Christ.

What lies ahead for our world in the next decade? More suffering. I'm sure of it. But to the extent that we become like the Magi, there is hope. To the extent that we plan and prepare for the Advent of Jesus, we can find peace. To the extent that we begin a journey where our paths cross His path, there will be joy. To the extent that we put into action the changes our encounter with this Holy One of God has had on our lives, love will abound, true love can be known, and the world can be changed.

I invite you now to journey through this Advent season with your heart open to receive Jesus. Use this book as a tool in your preparation for Christmas Day. It can be read in a single sitting. But as you will see, this book is best used as a daily companion as you journey with Jesus toward the day Christians set aside to celebrate the birthday of Jesus.

At the end of each day's devotion there is a section called "Advent Actions." These daily actions are provided as ideas of things you or your family can do to enhance your journey of discipleship and ministry to others, as you move toward Christmas Day. Most days have more than one "Advent Action," with the hopes you can find at least one to implement during Advent.

This book is simply a tool to help you, as you find your way through Advent. Tools are important. One reason we flail about spiritually during Advent is that we do not use any spiritual tools to help us on our journey. I'm delighted you've chosen this tool to assist you on your journey. For those of you who may be new to the concept of Advent as a spiritual discipline of preparing for Christmas Day, a historical sketch of Advent is offered in Appendix 1.

Now that you've discovered this tool, use it as a daily guide as you journey with the Magi toward Bethlehem. If you find it helpful, share it with a friend. We all need help finding our way.

Happy Advent and Merry Christmas.

Stanley's Shining Light
December 1

What would the Christmas story be without angels? Many years ago, a strange sounding angel was added to God's heavenly chorus. His name is Stanley. When I get to heaven, I fully expect to see Stanley Beaty singing in a heavenly chorus, and I expect to hear the same "errr" sound that he made as he praised God during his 47-year life.

I'll never forget the first time I saw Stanley. I was in the first grade eating my lunch with other members of my class. Stanley walked through the lunchroom with bird-like steps. He was an older teenager at that time. Each step he took seemed to take thought and determination. His back was arched, his eyes fixed straight ahead. He did not look at us as he passed by our table, but no doubt he heard the snickering from several of us as we laughed at his awkward crane-like steps.

Stanley was born with muscular dystrophy, a genetic disorder that involves a degenerative muscle weakness. Becker muscular dystrophy is carried on the X chromosome, which means that it affects only males. It may be transmitted by unaffected female carriers of the gene and transmitted to their sons. The sons of carriers each have a 50-50 chance of contracting the disease. The daughters of carriers each have a fifty-fifty chance of being carriers. Unbeknownst to Stanley's mother, Sybil, she was a carrier of the gene. Before Stanley was diagnosed with muscular dystrophy, she gave birth to two other sons, Howard and Tim. The odds went against these boys, too. All three were later diagnosed with the disease.

When I began attending Louisville Baptist Church as a pre-teen, I discovered the Beaty family was among the church's most faithful members. By this time, Stanley was in his early twenties. The disease had progressively worsened in his body, as well as in his younger brothers' bodies.

Upon arriving at church, I'd watch their father, William, carry Stanley's younger brother Tim, by this time the size of a grown man, on his back from the Beatys' car across the lawn and up the steps into the church. From there Tim would use his walker to get around. To watch the effort they went through to make it to church each Sunday was humbling. Years later, all three men would succumb to wheelchairs.

Stanley was nonverbal to most people. It was years before I ever heard him speak, but he was one of the first I heard sing in the worship service. The muscles he needed to force air from his lungs over his vocal cords were apparently not strong enough to create a normal tone. The sound that came out of his mouth was a high-pitched "errr." The sound was distinctive from the harmony of the other voices. Any visitor to the service would wonder about the origin of the sound that came from the front of the church. Stanley always sat on the second row from the front.

When I joined the youth choir, I was surprised that Stanley was there, even though he was past youth age. I often sat next to him in practice, feeling uncomfortable at first. Gradually, I came to look forward to seeing him. Later we became folder partners. I came to respect him greatly. Stanley taught me that anyone can sing praises to God and that God is not hung up on what one may sound like. God desires praise and adoration from one's heart. The Psalmist wrote: "Make a joyful noise unto God, all ye lands. Sing forth the honor of his name. Make his praise glorious" (Psalm 66:1-2 KJV).

The people of Louisville Baptist church learned to hear Stanley as God did, I think. His voice was a voice of praise, as were the others. I can't imagine how anyone in that church could have had any legitimate reason not to sing praises to God with Stanley there singing every week. Sometimes we forget to look at the heart, and we lose our way.

Stanley participated in our youth choir musical, "Lightshine," in the summer of 1975. As usual, no one in our church complained that Stanley's sound didn't harmonize with the rest of the choir. However, when we were invited to share the musical with another church, the choir director told Stanley she did not want him to sing. She was afraid his distinctive sound would be too much of a distraction for a church not acclimated to his voice.

Stanley didn't tell his family that he wasn't allowed to sing, so they showed up with Stanley. As the choir prepared to enter the guest church's sanctuary, Stanley stood in defiance at the front of the sanctuary facing the congregation, hoping to sing with the choir. His presence delayed the beginning of the service. He just stood there, back arched from his disease, face long with sadness, until his father came and led him away. We were singing a musical called "Lightshine," a musical about God's hope to the world, but Stanley was told that night he had to hide his light. His spirit was crushed. For a while, Stanley stopped attending church.

Over the years we watched helplessly as the disease overtook Stanley's body as well as his brothers. They each fought muscular dystrophy with a determination that would rival that of an Olympic athlete seeking to will his or her body to finish a marathon, especially Stanley. He was the last of the brothers to be confined to a wheelchair. He was the last of his brothers to die.

Once on my way back from college, I stopped by to see the Beatys. I had been by their home on other occasions to play dominoes, Stanley's favorite game. My purpose was to tell Stanley how much his presence at church and his singing had meant to me as a teenager. As a teenager, I was self-conscious about my small size, the need at that time to wear glasses, and the birthmark I had just above my hairline, which I kept covered up with my longer hairline in front. Then I'd sit beside Stanley at choir practice, and I'd feel ashamed that I ever complained about anything. I wanted Stanley to know that he ministered to me through those years, and that his life was a shining light to me.

His determination was surpassed only by that of his parents. For decades they cared for all three sons. For 47 years they cared for Stanley. Whenever I saw the parents arrive at church, and the van door opened, and each of their sons exited in his own wheelchair, I was reminded that despite the difficult circumstances they faced, they remained people of hope, people determined to serve God and worship God.

Whenever I hear people give reasons why they do not attend Bible study or worship services, I usually dismiss most of them as excuses. If anyone had reason to stay away from God's house, it was this family. If anyone had reason not to sing, it was Stanley. This family helped shape my faith. They helped me see it is not what's given to you that counts as much as it is what you make of what is given to you. This family made the most of what they were given. They gave the most of what they had.

As the choirs of heaven sing praises to God, I picture Stanley there singing. I don't think God has given him a perfect voice in heaven. I think the voice Stanley used here on earth is as distinctive in heaven as it was here. In fact, I have a feeling that from time to time, the angels may all stop singing and give Stanley a solo part. That "errr" sound comes from Stanley's heart. If we sing from our hearts, that's when worship occurs, and that's when God is praised. Otherwise, it's just music. As we find our way through this season of Advent, regardless of the difficulties life may present us, we can all find reasons to sing praises to God and reasons to let our light shine. Stanley taught me that.

Advent Actions

1. Light a candle in honor of someone significant whose light has helped push away some of the darkness in your life. If you choose, make this a family gathering and give each family member an opportunity to light a candle and share.

2. Make a list of times when people have made an impression on you by their actions instead of their words.

3. If you are prone to stay away from church and not worship with a community of believers, think about the excuses you typically use and compare them to the commitment of the Beaty family. How do you feel now about your excuses when compared to their commitment?

4. Sing or hum your favorite Christmas carol as your own private expression of worship to God.

5. Be intentional this Advent, and go to someone and tell the person what his or her example meant to you personally. Your words of affirmation may be one of the best gifts he or she receives this holiday season.

Prayer

God of Light,

The Apostle Paul wrote that You "chose what is foolish in the world to shame the wise...what is weak in the world to shame the strong... what is low and despised in the world... so that no human being might boast in the presence of God" (1 Corinthians 1:27-29 ESV).

God of Light, we are humbled by Stanley's life and by the commitment of his family to live their lives committed and dedicated to You, despite their daily hardships. Forgive those of us who are able bodied for making excuses, instead of being first in line to worship You in corporate worship and to serve You by serving others.

May others not have to wonder whether our light is shining. May they see it shining before they ever hear us speaking. May we embody the kind of gospel that Stanley embodied, the kind that was proposed by St. Francis of Assisi, who said: "Preach the gospel every day—sometimes use words." Amen.

Selfishness Can Trample the Life Out of Others
December 2

If we are not loving the Lord our God with all our hearts, with all our souls, with all our strength, and with all our minds and loving neighbors as ourselves (Luke 10:27), then it's very likely that we too are a part of a crowd that has our priorities all out of line during this Advent season.

It's hard to imagine being so hungry that people would step over crying, screaming children to get enough food for a single meal. This happened in Kanyaruchinya, Congo, Africa in 2008. I guess it's a human example of survival of the fittest. Yet it's also an example of how people's stomachs can overrule their hearts.

I realize I must be careful here. I have no idea what it's like to be on the brink of starvation. I would hope hunger wouldn't reduce me to the behavior of a savage, guilty of having the blood of children on the soles of my shoes, or the weight of their deaths weighing on my soul after I'd satisfied my hunger pains.

While I'll tread lightly in judging those in Kanyaruchinya, Congo, Africa, I cannot hold back in speaking of the trampling death of Jdimytai Damour in a Mineola, New York, Wal-Mart back in December of the same year. Mr. Damour was no small man. He tipped the scales at 270 pounds and was six feet, five inches tall. That's a lot of man! How can you not go around a man that size who is lying on the floor?

Police say Jdimytai, a 34-year-old temporary maintenance

worker, was pushed to the ground and asphyxiated when an esti-mated 2,000 shoppers broke through the glass doors at a Wal-Mart store on Long Island, the day after Thanksgiving, amid a bargain-hunting, frenzy-whipped crowd of shoppers.[3] He was steamrolled as these shoppers trampled him without any compassion as they head-ed to find low prices on television sets, computers, and other gifts, in the predawn hours that Friday morning.

It's hard to imagine people being so full of their selfish desire to acquire more stuff that they would trample a man. Most of the people who went through the checkout line in Wal-Mart that day likely spent less than $400. For $400, many of them helped stomp a man to death. They might as well have had rocks in their hands and stoned the man to death. What was his crime? He was in their way. He was between them and their house of toys. Jdimytai's tragedy is an example of how people's greed and desire for the material things of this world overruled their hearts.

It's an example of where people of our generation are placing their hope. Today, for a vast percentage of this world, hope is found in material things.

This incident draws quite a contrast between areas of Africa and America, between the Congo and Mineola, New York. While I think of the savagery of these two groups, how one group's stomachs and another group's greed led them to become group criminals, I must ask myself, "When does my selfishness tempt me to leave oth-ers behind—people who are wounded, battered, and bleeding? How does my selfishness contribute to another's loss of hope?"

Perhaps someone else struck the initial blow. Perhaps I saw the need, but refused to get involved. Getting involved, after all, would be costly. Like the priest and the Levite in Jesus' story of the Good Samaritan, both perhaps with busy schedules and important religious functions to perform, I sometimes move on my way, leav-ing the wounded for others to care for, or maybe no one at all. Dare I confess that I sometimes am the one who steps on others to get what I want?

Wal-Mart tells us to come shop at their stores so we can save money and live better. Jesus tells us if we want to live better, we need to look to see where our treasure is because there we will find our hearts. It seems that Jesus wants us to find treasure in others as opposed to finding treasure in material things, accolades, or power. We should treasure and value each person we meet, seeing ourselves in them. If we were in their place, how would we like to be treated? Once we've answered that question, then we should treat people like that as opposed to seeing people as obstacles in our way. If we contribute in some way, either directly or indirectly to people being stepped on, bruised and wounded because of treasure that we seek, then we've lost our way.

If we are not loving the Lord our God with all our hearts, with all our souls, with all our strength, and with all our minds, and loving neighbors as ourselves (Luke 10:27), then it's very likely that we are also a part of a crowd that has lost our way during this Advent season.

Advent Actions

1. Make a donation to a local food bank. Better yet, volunteer your time at a local food bank or shelter.

2. Become aware of the products you purchase. Do you know who makes them? Do you know where they are made and under what conditions? Would you stop buying the product if you knew it was made by child labor or under conditions where people are abused or mistreated?

3. Make a contribution to an African relief agency. The "Bricks for Ricks Liberian Housing Foundation" was established in 2009 to help provide housing for those displaced from the civil war in Liberia and as a support for Ricks Institute, a Baptist school in Virginia, Liberia for grades 1-12. Contributions to Bricks for Ricks Liberian Housing Foundation, Inc., can be mailed to: Jefferson First Baptist Church, 81 Institute Street, Jefferson, GA 30549. (See www.thefaithlab.com/advent for links.)

4. Today when you eat, give God thanks for sufficient food in your home.

5. As you go on your way through Advent, look for an opportunity to allow others to go ahead of you. Practice hospitality. Jesus said:

> The greatest among you should be like the youngest,
> and the one who rules like the one who serves. For who
> is greater, the one who is at the table or the one who
> serves? Is it not the one who is at the table? But I am

among you as one who serves. You are those who have
stood by me in my trials (Luke 22:26-28).

6. Identify those times you have stepped on others to get what you wanted. Seek forgiveness.

Prayer

God of the Least of These,

Like your disciples, we have clamored for the best seats. Forgive us for the times we have lost sight of loving others in an effort to love ourselves.

Forgive us for those times we've run over others to acquire attention, or possessions, or to satisfy our selfish desires.

God of the Least of These, help us to step away from a crowd that's hell-bent on going in a direction that's opposed to your teachings. May we be the ones willing to embody the prophetic voices, even though those who speak out sometimes pay a price for speaking the truth, for "how beautiful are the feet of those who bring good news!" (Romans 10:15). May we have beautiful feet, Lord, not feet that walk over people, but feet that walk to people carrying them the love of Christ. Amen.

Learning Grace Under My Grandparents' Pecan Trees
December 3

For many years during my boyhood, I lived beside my grandparents. They had about fifteen pecan trees that lined the road and surrounded their house. The tall branches provided wonderful shade each summer from the scorching heat. I learned to love those trees, not just for the shade they provided but also for the promise of money that would come my way during the fall. Like a soldier, I guarded the trees from invading woodpeckers with my BB gun. My father built me a tree house in one of them, which served as a great lookout tower for blue jays or squirrels that might be tempted to sneak in and rob me of my crop. (As a boy growing up on a farm, I didn't have much guilt about shooting birds. Today, I enjoy bird watching of all kinds.)

Even though the trees were not mine, nor the pecans that fell in the fall, I came to think of them as mine because of the generosity of my grandparents. I could keep the money from all the pecans I gathered and sold. As I grew older, I became more efficient in gathering the pecans. I learned which kind of pecan brought the most money. For example, Stuarts sold for more than Seedlings.

I learned the most efficient method of gathering the pecans. First, I raked the yards free of leaves and sticks. Once the preparation was done, I'd call the man who operated the pecan shaker to come and shake the trees. I could feel my pockets filling with money as the long arm of the machine rose to meet the big strong arms of the trees. With a rat-a-tat-tat, the trees shook like dancers on "Soul Train," and the sky began to rain money. The sound of pecans falling by the thousands, some hitting the tin roof of the house, made me feel as if I'd hit an oil gusher. Dollar signs flashed in my eyes. I danced around the yard singing, "I'm in the money! I'm in the money!"

One year during the Advent season, this process had just been completed. The tree shaker had just left the yard. There wasn't a place in the yard you could step without stepping on pecans. Then, unexpectedly, my cousins from out of state showed up. After the hugs and the greetings, my grandmother said to them, "Why don't you children grab a bucket and go help Michael pick up pecans and make you a little Christmas money?"

I was not happy! I was greedy. I wanted every pecan for myself. I'd prepared the yard. I'd paid for the shaking of the trees. It didn't seem fair that my cousins could waltz in and share in the harvest. Of course, I didn't stop to think that the pecans weren't even mine to begin with.

My experience with the pecan trees reminds me of a parable Jesus once told about a man, who owned a vineyard. He found men to work in his vineyard at the beginning of the day, and they agreed on a wage. About every three hours he went out into the marketplace and found others to come work in his vineyard, agreeing with them that he would pay them whatever was fair. Just one hour before the twelve-hour workday was over, he found more workers. At the end of the day, all the workers were paid for their work. He began paying the workers who worked the least amount of time, one hour. Surprisingly, they were given a full day's wage. As it turned out, all the workers, right up to the ones who had worked a twelve-hour day, received a full day's wage.

Those who worked the longest were not happy, even though they had received exactly what they agreed to work for. They didn't think it was fair that those who came in at the last minute should be given the same wage as those who had worked all day. When the vineyard owner was questioned about this, he responded:

> *Friend, I am not being unfair to you. Didn't you agree to work for a denarius? Take your pay and go. I want to give the man who was hired last the same as I gave you. Don't I have the right to do what I want with my own money? Or are you envious because I am generous? (Matthew 20:14-15).*

On that winter afternoon among the pecans of my grandparents' backyard, I felt like those in Jesus' parable who had worked all day and received the same wage as those who had worked only one hour. I didn't feel there was justice in the situation.

From my grandparents' perspective, they owned the trees. The pecans were theirs. They had agreed only that I could have all I picked up. My grandparents easily made room for the coming of my cousins, their beloved grandchildren, and desired that they fill their buckets with the bounty that covered the ground.

I was already receiving what was promised to me, the opportunity to earn money from trees that were not mine. Even so, I was still envious of my grandparents' generosity to others. I wish I could say the lesson sunk in that day, but it didn't. I directed my cousins to the area of the Seedlings (a smaller pecan that brings less money at the market) and I went to the area where the Stuarts were. The generosity of my grandparents had not yet become a part of my nature.

During Advent, the Lord desires that we make room in our hearts for those who arrive in our lives unannounced. Their arrival will cost us something. They may be the beneficiaries of our hard work. They may receive more than we think they should have based on the amount of work they did. We never know where these people will come from, how many will come, or how often. But during

Advent, don't be surprised when someone shows up who you believe doesn't deserve the blessings of the season or certainly not a full share. When that moment comes, you can respond as most people would, and as I did with my cousins, with great restraint.

There is another approach. If we learn anything from the coming of the Christ Child, we should learn that among the greatest gifts we receive are those we do not deserve. It becomes easier to be the giver of grace when we stop and remember we have been the recipients of amazing grace, the kind of grace that saves sinners, greedy sinners who in times of plenty tend to forget the source of our blessings. We can easily slip into the belief that we are somehow entitled to the gift of Christ. None of us are.

Paul wrote to the Ephesians:

God saved you by his special favor when you believed. And you can't take credit for this; it is a gift from God. Salvation is not a reward for the good things we have done, so none of us can boast about it (Ephesians 2:8-9 NLT).

May this thought help you find your way as you move through Advent. Just as important, by your keeping the grace of God in mind during Advent, it is likely that God will use you to help others have hope as you help them find their way.

Advent Actions

1. Make a pecan pie for a friend, and give a copy of this book as a gift.

Here's Mrs. Janie Johnson's recipe for pecan pie:

Ingredients
1 cup sugar
1 teaspoon vanilla
¾ cup white corn syrup
1 cup chopped pecans
½ stick margarine
Dash of salt
3 eggs, lightly beaten
1 (10-inch) pie shell, baked

Directions
Preheat oven to 350°F. Mix sugar, syrup and margarine. Bring to boil. Boil three minutes. Pour slowly over very lightly beaten eggs. Add vanilla and salt. Pour into pie shell. Bake 40-50 minutes at 350°F or until firm in center. Serves 8.

2. Order a gift tin, a gift basket, or a one-pound bag of pecans from the Louisville Pecan Company in my hometown of Louisville, Alabama to give to a friend. Practice a little grace and send a gift of pecans to someone who doesn't deserve them. (See www.thefaithlab. com/advent for a link to Louisville Pecan Company.)

3. It's possible that people will show up unexpectedly at your house during Advent. Begin now to prepare for their arrival. Ask God to help you be a gracious host, even if you aren't all that excited about seeing them. Prepare some small inexpensive gifts to give to these people who stop by.

4. Write a prayer thanking God for the grace you have received.

5. Write a letter to someone thanking him/her for grace he/she extended to you in a particular situation or period in your life.

Prayer

God of Grace,

We come to You not because we are entitled, but because You have invited us into Your presence. Each of us has experienced Your grace. None of us deserves Your grace, love or forgiveness.

We confess that we sometimes march into Your presence as if we are entitled and lay claim to Your love as if we earned it, much like the man who was hired to work in the vineyard first. He worked and received his fair wage, but then he was angry because he discovered You had extended grace to others who had not worked as long and as hard.

The problem with us, Lord, is that we are more like those people being hired late, receiving grace from You for that which we didn't earn, yet thinking we are more like the man who has worked a full day and earned every good thing we have coming.

Therefore, Lord, during Advent, help us be people who live with a spirit of thanksgiving. As we remember where our gifts come from, help us to be more giving to others. Help us treat others with grace, extending warmth when they offer us a cold shoulder, a smile when they give us a piercing stare, and kind words when they prick us with stabbing remarks. May we be Christ to those who make us carry their load by going with them the extra mile. Amen.

Santa Claus
Is Semper Fidelis
December 4

My son John spent four years in the U.S. Marine Corps. The graduation ceremony at Parris Island was very impressive. The field on which the First Battalion marched was the same field where Marines have trained for battles in places like the Pacific islands, Korea, Vietnam, Kuwait, Iraq, and Afghanistan.

Few graduating classes, if any, are spared battles. Perhaps one day our nation will be at peace with the world. Better said, perhaps the world will be at peace with us. For now, they rage on. Yet on graduation day, Marines bask in their accomplishments.

Having just completed the Crucible, 54 straight hours of no sleep, where recruits' endurance is tested, and teamwork and skills are pushed to the limit, the recruits were filled with pride, emotion, and a sense of accomplishment as at no other time in their lives. As the Emblem, Globe, and Anchor pins were pinned to the collars of the graduates, some graduates allowed tears of joy to roll down their dirt-caked faces.

The Marine band played, cannons fired, drill instructors barked their last commands to these recruits as they marched in perfect unison onto the parade field. As if invited to the ceremony, a bald eagle circled the parade field, as if it were giving its blessing to the entire morning's procession.

More than one million Marines have trained at Parris Island. Blood, sweat, and tears have been left there. Boys have been fashioned into men and girls into women as much as humanly possible in a three-month period. Friendships have been forged that have lasted lifetimes. Hatred for drill instructors has been forged there, too, which seems to later morph into a mixture of awe and respect.

John's graduation was a great day of celebration for our family. With the forthcoming graduation from high school of our younger son Ryan, who was soon to be off to the University of Tennessee on a diving scholarship, my wife and I took the day in with great joy.

That Christmas we knew was one to savor as we drove our sons home. Who knew what the holiday of the future might bring? What parts of the world might John be called to serve? Would we be together in the Christmases to come?

As we passed through Tifton on our way home from Parris Island, our young men wanted to stop at the mall. There was one store there they wanted to check out. The mall in Tifton, Georgia isn't much of a mall. Nevertheless, Santa had managed to find it and had set up an impressive island there to talk to children and to have photos taken.

The only problem: Santa wasn't getting much business. In my day, the lines were long. You had to wait at least thirty minutes to an hour to see Santa, and by the time you got to him you forgot half of what was on your list. As I remember, Santa didn't seem too patient to let you sit there on his knee forever to think about the other items. As you said, "And ah, and ah," Santa was quick to finish your sentence with "And lots of surprises?" Then he said, "Ho, Ho, Ho" and "Merry Christmas," set you down, handed you a candy cane, patted you on the head and handed you back to a parent who led you away as Santa had another child set down on his lap. At that very moment you usually thought of the other items.

The Santa in the Tifton mall could have played a few hands of solitaire or made good use of the video functions on a cell phone. There were no long lines, which may explain why he had time to wave at me. I waved back. He looked like the Santa I believe in. His beard looked real. His belly was full.

I said, "Hey, Ryan, let's get a family picture made with Santa." My younger son looked at me like I'd just suggested we go to Chucky Cheese and play video games—with his girlfriend. "Nooo," he said. "Ah, come on," I said, "Santa looks lonely. Besides, when's the next time we'll all be together for something like this?"

When Tina and John joined us, I asked again. Now, Ryan knew I was serious. We all had on red shirts because red was the Marine's color of choice for graduation that day. We even brought a red shirt for John to change into from his military uniform.

How long had it been—maybe twelve or thirteen years—since my sons had met with Santa? Certainly long enough to know that nothing's magical anymore about a plump, bearded man in a red suit. That was about to change.

As we walked onto Santa's wonderland island, Santa told each of us where we should sit. Tina sat on his left. I sat on his right. Ryan knelt down in front of Tina. John knelt down in front of me. Two pictures were taken. As we stood up Santa looked at John and said, "Son, you look like you are just coming back from boot camp."

Surprised at Santa's intuition, John said, "Yes, sir. I just finished my training at Parris Island, and I graduated today."

Santa shook John's hand and said, "Semper Fi, (The Marine motto that means "Always Faithful"), Parris Island 1969." Santa was a Marine!

With a look of shock, probably wondering where Santa kept his reindeer while he trained, John said, "No way. They say you meet a Marine almost everywhere you go." Now, he knew it was true. For the next five minutes, I listened to my son and Santa compare the differences in recruit training from 1969 to 2007.

As Santa said his goodbyes, he shook John's hand one last time. He called attention to his smooth white gloves. "You might recognize these," he said. "These are the gloves I wore with my Dress Blues." It was probably the only part of the uniform that still fit.

Before we left, Santa gave us all a candy cane. Strange thing, though, Santa never asked any of us what we wanted for Christmas. I guess Santa already knew. He had given us what most families need, the memory of being together and a picture in our minds that will last a lifetime. We left with our hearts filled with joy and love for one another. What more could Santa bring?

Advent Actions

1. Regardless of the ages of the members of your family, make a trip to the local mall and have a family picture made with Santa. Choose a color for everyone to wear in the photo.

2. Find out who will have a relative missing during the holidays because he or she is in the military and will be unable to take leave to return home. Find a creative way to minister to this family.

3. Remember, it's not stuff that makes the season memorable; it's the experiences. Notice, the story isn't about what my sons stopped by the mall to purchase. Sometimes experiences just happen, but sometimes they are planned. What can you plan for your family during Advent, that's not expensive, that could become a talking point for years to come?

Prayer

Semper Fidelis God,

Your faithfulness to us is never ending. We are reminded of your faithfulness in the accomplishments of our children and in the promise their lives hold. When we first set them on Santa's lap, until the day they are reluctant to go, you remain faithful.

When we rush to the mall with our lists in hand, fight the traffic, and lose our tempers in the midst of all the stress, we forget what the season is truly all about. Yet, you remain faithful.

When we lose the sense of wonder about the Advent season and refuse to acknowledge the little child within us, you remain faithful.

You remain faithful to nudge us toward finding our inner child, and not allow a world where there are a lot of serious things taking place, like Marines training for war, people jockeying for places on the interstate, and people being treated for cancer, to cause us to lose our love for a season, where wonder is the prelude, miracle is the story line, and awe is the postlude.

Though the birth of Christ happened long ago, we look today for new signs that you are working among us. So, thank you for this example: Santa, a Marine. While we need our Marines and other branches of the armed forces to keep our nation safe and free, when they can lay down their weapons, hold their children, and entertain their families, then Lord, some of the hope we have waited for will have arrived. Send us peace, Lord. Amen.

There's a Bad Apple in My Family Tree
December 5

My great-great-great-grandfather was Robert E. Lee, not General Robert E. Lee, but Corporal Robert Edward Lee. At the age of forty he enlisted in the Confederate Army. He was a member of the 29th Alabama Infantry Regiment. He was wounded twice in the war and was once cited for bravery. He was among a group of soldiers detached for service to oppose the invasion of Mobile toward the end of the war. These men ended up surrendering at Citronelle, Alabama in April 1865. After being turned over to General Sam Jones in Tallahassee, Florida, they were taken to Albany, Georgia, where they were released at the end of the war.

After the war, Robert Lee settled in Barbour County, Alabama. He married Mary Pary Parmer, and they had four children. After her death, Robert Lee married again. He married Ida E. Griffin. The eyebrow-raising thing about this marriage was that Robert Lee was sixty-five and Ida Griffin was sixteen.

Oops. Just when you think you've got a good apple in the family tree, out pops a worm. There's no indication that Robert Lee ever regretted his marriage to Ida, but "I'da" wished he had been a bit younger or she had been a bit older. It's a little shameful to find something like that in your family tree. He served honorably as a brave soldier in the Civil War, but in his later years my great-great-great-granddaddy Lee was guilty of robbing the cradle, in the worst sort of way.

I bet if you do a little climbing up your family tree, you are bound to find a bad apple or two. Even Jesus had a few bad apples in his family tree. Have you ever looked at the family tree of Jesus? Matthew and Luke record Jesus' genealogy, which is traced through Joseph, as it was the custom to trace one's lineage through the male in those days, which is sort of interesting since Joseph didn't have anything to do with Jesus' conception.

If you compare the two genealogies, you will discover that they are not exactly alike. And if you accept the Christian contention that Jesus was born of a virgin, which I hope you do, then these genealogies must have been written to tell us something other than from whom Jesus descended. Here are two explanations and maybe a little proof that some good theology lies buried in all of those "begats" after all.

By tracing Jesus' ancestry, Matthew and Luke communicate that Jesus has always been a part of God's plan. Luke communicates this by tracing Jesus' genealogy back to Adam, whom he referred to as the "Son of God." Matthew goes back only as far as Abraham, but in the process he actually points out some of the bad apples in Jesus' family tree. Interesting.

He begins by naming Tamar, who was a widow. By law, her deceased husband's brother was supposed to have married her, so that she would have a home and be able to have children. However, her father-in-law Judah would not bless such a union. She waited for years for Judah to keep his word that he'd allow his youngest son to marry her.

When it finally became evident that he was not going to keep his word, Tamar became so desperate that she posed as a prostitute and traded her services for Judah's seal, cord, and staff. She became pregnant and was going to be stoned for her actions, but she proved that Judah was the father of her child by producing his seal, cord, and staff. Unable to deny his sin, Judah repented for his actions and also for failing to allow his son to marry Tamar, which the law demanded. He realized that, indirectly, he was responsible for her actions. Tamar gave birth to twins. One was Perez, an ancestor of Jesus.

The second interesting person in Jesus' family tree is Rahab, a woman who lived in the city of Jericho. Her house was built into the city wall. She lived there with her mother, father, and brothers. It appears that she had children.

Rahab was also a prostitute. In the days in which Rahab lived, women were not treated well. It's very possible that her family forced her into prostitution to make money for the family.

Many people live lifestyles today in which they feel trapped and have little hope. They are extremely unhappy with how they are living, but they wake up each day and ask the question, "What choice do I have?" They think, "I either work this job I hate, or I don't eat. If I don't listen and do what he says, he might hit me again. If I don't pay the high interest rate, they are going to take my car."

Perhaps Rahab invited men into her bed with the same kind of desperation. It's quite possible she hated herself for what she did.

Have you ever hated yourself for something you've done, for past mistakes? Have you had problems overcoming guilt, forgiving yourself, and moving forward with a new focus?

Rahab's life changed the day some Israeli spies came into Jericho. These spies were casing out the city and were going to take a report back to Joshua about the best means to attack it. The spies went under cover with Rahab. Well, not literally.

They found out where the prostitute lived and went there thinking their presence at such a place would draw the least amount of attention from the locals, but they were wrong. The king found out about the Israelites and sent some of his men to arrest them. However, Rahab lied. She said the spies left at dusk, when actually she had hidden them under stalks of flax on the roof.

These spies didn't bring Rahab any business, but they brought

her hope because the reputation of their God had preceded them.
She said to them:

> *I know that the LORD has given this land to you and*
> *that a great fear of you has fallen on us, so that all*
> *who live in this country are melting in fear because*
> *of you. We have heard how the LORD dried up the*
> *water of the Red Sea for you when you came out*
> *of Egypt, and what you did to Sihon and Og, the two*
> *kings of the Amorites east of the Jordan, whom you*
> *completely destroyed. When we heard of it, our hearts*
> *melted and everyone's courage failed   because of you,*
> *for the LORD your God is God in heaven above and*
> *on the earth below. Now then, please swear to me by*
> *the LORD that you will show kindness to my fam-*
> *ily, because I have shown kindness to you. Give me a*
> *sure sign that you will spare the lives of my father and*
> *mother, my brothers and sisters, and all who belong*
> *to them, and that you will save us from death (Joshua*
> *2:9-13).*

When the Israelites destroyed Jericho, Rahab and all her
family were the only ones saved. As she was told, she tied a scarlet
cord in the window through which she let the men down to escape.
It was the sign to let her and her family live.

The writer of Hebrews wrote that Rahab was a woman of
faith (Hebrews 11:31). James wrote: "Was not even Rahab the prostitute considered righteous for what she did when she gave lodging
to the spies and sent them off in a different direction?" (James 2:25).

The third out-of-place member of Jesus' family tree is Ruth.
She is mentioned in Matthew's family tree. Ruth was far from being
a bad apple, except for the fact that she was not Jewish. She was a
Moabite. That made her a bad apple, not to mention a non-Jew in a

Jew's family tree.

Ruth's story begins when there was a famine in Bethlehem and Elimelech and Naomi, two Israelites, moved with their two sons to Moab. Both sons married Moabite women. One of their sons married Ruth. But tragedy came to Naomi. Her husband died, and then both of her sons died. She was left in a foreign land with two daughters-in-law. Too old to remarry, she decided to go back to Bethlehem, where she had some family, but told her daughters-in-law to stay, marry, and have a family. But Ruth refused to stay. She said: "Don't urge me to leave you or to turn back from you. Where you go I will go, and where you stay I will stay. Your people will be my people and your God my God" (Ruth 1:16-17).

The chances of a foreign woman moving to Bethlehem and finding a husband were not good. Who would have ever thought that Ruth would fall in love with a relative of Naomi who would have mutual feelings for her? But that's what happened. This relative's name was Boaz.

The two became husband and wife and gave birth to a child named Obed. Obed became the father of Jesse, who was the father of the man who became the greatest king of Israel, David, whose family line leads straight to Jesus.

Do you have someone of another country, race, or ethnic origin in your family? Do you have someone from another region of the country who seems like a foreigner in your family? Families can become complex organisms. People from different races, cultures, and geographical settings do fall in love. It presents unique challenges, which we have to work through.

Jews would not have wanted it broadcast that Gentiles were a part of their heritage. Yet Matthew points this out. Matthew wrote for a Jewish readership. He found it important to remind those who were often prejudiced toward Gentiles that Jesus had some Gentile ancestors.

Matthew also mentions Bathsheba, except he does not call her by name. Instead he says that "David was the father of Solomon, whose mother had been Uriah's wife" (Matthew 1:6). This could have been worded differently. In fact, Matthew could have omitted mentioning this terrible sin by David, just as he could have avoided mentioning the sins of Tamar and Judah. He did not have to mention that Jesus' ancestors had mixed blood. Why point out the bad apples?

Perhaps Matthew wants the reader to see David as a King with a tainted legacy. He does this by referring to the sin he committed with Bathsheba.

In showing these bad apples, Matthew reminds us that Jesus had in his genealogy people who made some poor sexual and ethical decisions. (David instructed his general to have Bathsheba's husband sent to the front lines so he would be killed.)

By reading Matthew, people who have made similar choices can see there is hope for them. You may struggle with guilt from past relationships. You may have made poor choices years ago because you felt trapped, and you may still feel you are paying for those decisions.

Regardless, the Good News is that Jesus has a plan to heal you from being broken. Jesus has arms big enough to wrap around you. You see, Jesus' own mother, the last female listed in the family tree of Jesus, conceived a child by the Holy Spirit while she was pledged to be married. Even Jesus' own mother, Mary, had to deal with the scorn and the ridicule of those who felt she had sinned, even though she had not. Had it not been for an angel coming to Joseph in a dream, he would never have married her. He never would have believed how she conceived Jesus. He didn't want to expose her to public disgrace, but he would have quietly set her aside.

Matthew's gospel says that Jesus was called "Immanuel," which means "God with us." One thing Tamar, Rahab, Ruth,

Bathsheba, and Mary had in common is that God was with them. Despite their sins and the sins of the men around them and problems they faced, God was with them. God did not forsake them. And God was with Mary throughout her pregnancy and life.

Through Jesus, God chose to identify with the human race, in spite of our sinfulness. In the lineage of Jesus are both rich heritage and sinful people. Yet God worked through both to bring about his plan. God took the good branches and the bad ones and made them grow into a tree that gave us the Son of God, the second Adam, Jesus.

It is good news that through Jesus, God chose to identify with the human race, even though we all have less than perfect heritages and will leave a less than perfect legacy. Through the coming of Jesus, we all have an opportunity to be grafted into the tree of life. The tree of life, which Jesus represents, stands tall with its branches and reaches far enough for anyone who desires to come under its shade. The best legacy we can leave for future generations is a witness of a life lived attached to the tree of life.

Most people erect a tree in their homes during Advent and adorn it with ornaments and lights. As you do so this year, think of the family tree of Jesus. Think of your own tree of faith. Are you grafted into Christ's family tree of faith? Remember, nothing you have done can keep you from becoming a part of this great heritage, except refusing to accept the coming of the Lord into your life.

When future generations work on their genealogies and your name comes up on one of the branches, I pray you will have lived in such a way that you will have shown generations that come after you the way to the manger, the cross, and the empty tomb. Even if our lives are marked by some terrible tragedy or sin, Matthew's family tree of Jesus is proof that those events or sins do not have to be the defining marks of our lives. The defining marks of our lives can be found in the scars of Christ on the cross. Our sins were buried with

Him. New life for us was raised in Him. Praise God, Jesus has shown us the way.

Advent Actions

1. Contact members of your family and find out if anyone has done any family genealogical work. Old family Bibles are good places to begin to discover if there is any recorded information. Begin to collect the basic information about your family history.

2. Make an effort to visit the oldest member of your family or one of the oldest. Ask that person to tell some stories, good or bad, about members of the family who are now living or deceased. Find out something about the faith history. What did your relatives believe about God, and what kind of faith was handed down to the next generation? Ask where those people are buried. If your relative is able, plan a trip to gravesites of deceased relatives. In some cases, these gravesites are in rural areas of old churches.

   Suggestion: Make a video recording of your conversation with your relative. These stories about past generations are going to go to the grave with your kin if they are not told and preserved.

3. One of the most extensive deposits of genealogical records is housed at the Ellen Payne Odom Genealogical Library in Moultrie, Georgia. (See the link at www.faithlab.com/advent.)

4. Read Matthew's genealogy of Jesus. Notice the names in Jesus' family tree. Recall as many biblical stories of these people as possible. As you do, remember that while many of them had many positive qualities, the Bible also lists their many sins. Jesus had less than a perfect heritage, as do we. We will also have less than a perfect heritage, and we will leave a less than perfect one. Nevertheless, ask

God to help you set the right kind of example, so that when other generations look back, your life will be an example of faith and commitment to God. Thankfully, Jesus left us a perfect example to follow.

Prayer

God of All Generations and All People Groups,

The Hebrews addressed You as the God of Abraham, Isaac, and Jacob, as a way of acknowledging that You journeyed with their ancestors. We too acknowledge that You are a God who has journeyed with those who have come before us. We know You in part because of the testimonies of those who have come before us. Because You continue to be faithful in being Immanuel (God with us), we want future generations to know of our faith and dependence on You. May our lives reflect that commitment.

When the history of our generation is written, Lord, and oral history is shared about us and our names appear in the records of someone's family tree, may we be known by our legacy of faith, evidenced by our benevolent acts in our communities, our commitment to our family, and our witness of Christ through Your Church and world. Amen.

Finding Faith
in the Heavens
December 6

My internal clock woke me about five minutes before the alarm was set to sound. It's amazing how the body will do that, especially since the time I set the clock was 3:25 A.M. I dressed, prepared some hot chocolate and then woke my 12-year-old son, Ryan. I wasn't excited to be awake at that time of the morning and neither was he.

We drove over to the home our friends, the Russells. David and his son, Jacob, had invited us to come over and sit out under the stars and watch the sky. We had been promised by the experts to be treated to a meteor shower, and we were not disappointed.

It was like a fireworks show on the Fourth of July. Little streaks of light randomly raced across the night sky, several every minute. Occasionally, one left a tracer, like those left from the firing of anti-aircraft guns against the blackness of night, as we've seen on television during wartime.

"Look, Ryan, look!" I said at one point. "I see it! I see it!" he said. "It's going to crash into the earth!" The ball of fire in the sky was unlike anything I had ever seen. The comet-like streak lasted for several seconds and was easily the largest of the Leonid meteors we saw streak across the sky. It was incredible! We soon forgot that we were sacrificing sleep. We were having too much fun experiencing part of God's world with which we were far too unfamiliar. It's a shame that we aren't more intentional about introducing our children to more of God's world.

A few days later, I went fishing with one of my church members, Mr. Jack Hall. I took him out onto his pond on my new Gheenoe. It's a slick little boat made for ponds, rivers, and the ocean flats. He told me about the time he and a friend floated down the river, all the way to the ocean from Moultrie. It took them a week. "How old were you, Mr. Jack?" "We were sixteen," he said. "I don't guess teenagers do much of that anymore," he said. It made me think of Tom Sawyer and Huckleberry Finn. "No, I don't think there are very many mothers who would allow their teenage sons to float down a river like that these days," I said.

That conversation with Mr. Hall made me wish for simpler days, when boys could explore the outdoors like that. A sense of wonder is the beginning of knowledge, and the best place for that sense of wonder to germinate is in nature. We don't take the time to study what's above us, beneath us, or around us anymore. We spend too much of our time in front of the television or with electronic devices. We don't know the names of the trees, plants, insects, or the constellations of the stars. Space exploration originally began because people wondered enough about the cosmos to watch it and ultimately explore it.

It's really a sign of our arrogance that we don't take more interest in the activities of this universe. As long as the earth rotates to allow the sun to shine on us another day, there are too many of us who care little about what happens around us or what happens in the heavens, even though our existence is tied to them.

There are exceptions. I'll never forget Brian Gray, a young man who grew up in Moultrie, Georgia. He's passionate about the heavens. His interest was first sparked in 1997 with the appearance of the comet Hale-Bopp. He owns a Celestron C8 telescope, which gives him the ability to see deep into space. He has learned how to use his telescope to photograph space activity, a process known as astrophotography.

Several years ago, Brian captured two incredible images on film. One is a photograph of the Trifid Nebula, which contains hundreds of thousands of stars. What was particularly exciting about his photograph is that he captured a star in the process of birth. Brian explained to me that stars are born when huge clouds of molecular hydrogen attract pieces of matter. As the matter comes closer and closer together, occupying smaller and smaller space, pressure inside the space increases, and the temperature rises to the point where it can sustain a thermonuclear reaction, and the star is born. If you don't understand that, don't worry; neither do I.

Ironically, the other photograph Brian captured was that of a dying star within the Dumbbell Nebula. Brian explained that as hydrogen in the star is converted to helium, the star eventually creates less heat, gravity crushes the star, and it collapses in on itself. The star implodes and then explodes the gas. For Brian, his experience in astronomy has served the purpose of confirming the faith he was taught as a child.

The heavens helped confirm the Psalmist's faith too. Seeing the stars and heavens was a daily occurrence for the Psalmist David. Living out on the open land, tending his sheep, he used the stars for navigation, for light, and to ponder the very existence of God.

It prompted him to write these words:

> The heavens declare the glory of God, the skies proclaim the work of his hands. Day by day they pour forth speech; night after night they display knowledge. There is no speech or language where their voice is not heard. Their voice goes out into all the earth and the word to the ends of the earth (Psalm 19:1-3).

As Brian Gray pondered the creation of the universe through

the existing and changing material properties of space, he concluded that everything has to have a beginning point. "Matter doesn't just come from nothing," he said. Looking through a telescope has been a religious experience for him, helping him affirm that God is the force behind all creation, both past and present.

From the broadcast of the Discovery Space Shuttle on November 1, 1998, astronaut John Glenn said:

> *I don't think you can be up here and look out the window as I did the first day and see the earth from this vantage point, to look out at this kind of creation and not believe in God. To me, it's impossible—it just strengthens my faith. I wish there were words to describe what it's like.*[4]

The heavens do, indeed, declare the glory of God.

It's the job of Christianity to say that God is the source of all creation, that matter exists because God created the universe out of nothing, which is the way we are told it was done in the book of Genesis. It's the job of science to study the properties of matter and space, and determine how God may have done it and how God is still doing it. The two disciplines do not have to be incompatible.

With anything that science is able to prove about the universe and about the origins of life, we can simply thank God for taking His hand and pulling back the veil of mystery, just a little for us, to see how it was done. Good science does not threaten the faith of the Christian, and honest Christianity does not cast aside good science; nor does Christianity allow bad science to speak without accountability.

Scientists are taught to believe in what they can see and objectively prove. However, good science and faith in God do not have to be opposites. The physicist Charles Townes, a 1964 Nobel Prize winner, wrote:

Science wants to know the mechanism of the universe, religion the meaning. Many scientists feel there is no place in research for discussion of anything that sounds mystical. But it's unreasonable to think we already know enough about the natural world to be confident about the totality of forces.[5]

We expect scientists to base their data on research and data. However, those seeking verifiable data can also ask questions of meaning, which cannot be scientifically verified.

Here's a news flash! The universe is so big that we will never stop learning about it because the universe is a reflection of its creator; therefore, there will be parts of it that will always be shrouded in mystery. That should never stop us from asking difficult questions, seeking answers, and trying to uncover the mysteries of the universe.

My experience looking at the Leonid meteor shower with my son was a holy experience. As I lay there on a sleeping bag looking up at the heavens, I thought of people long ago who had an intimate relationship with the starry skies of night. They did not have the advantage of using high-powered telescopes to look deep into space, but they did not need one to be awed by its expanse and mystery, and humbled by the beauty of unknown worlds.

The Psalmist wrote: "When I consider your heavens, the work of your fingers, the moon and the stars, which you have ordained, what is man that you are mindful of him, and the son of man that you visit him?" (Psalm 8:3-4 NKJV).

Had the Psalmist had access to all the scientific information we have today about the heavens, would he be any more awed by what God has created or any more humbled that God chooses to notice us and enter into a relationship with us? I think not. In fact, I think his scientific knowledge would only serve to increase his awe of God and his humility that we are so highly thought of in God's universe.

It shouldn't surprise us that the night sky could be such an important point of discovery of faith for people. Two thousand years ago astrologers were guided to Judea by a star because they believed it symbolized that a king had been born, and if they followed it, they would find him.

Was it good science or great faith that carried them to the manger? Following a star through the darkness required some skill and some faith.

You and I must travel through dark days in this life. Right now, you may be experiencing some dark days. To navigate them, you need both wisdom and faith. Both of these can lead to hope.

During Advent, remember, the Bible tells us that Jesus is "the bright Morning Star" (Revelation 22:16). Remember, God gave Solomon wisdom when he asked.

Take a little time this Advent season to do a little star gazing, literally. Reflect on the vastness of God's universe. Marvel at how God would unite a star in the heavens with a birth on the earth, and use it as His compass for men willing to place their faith in a mysterious God. They found their way through the darkness using their minds and their hearts.

So, join with the Psalmist who wrote: "When I consider your heavens, the work of your fingers, the moon and the stars, which you have set in place, what is man that you are mindful of him, the son of man that you care for him?" (Psalm 8:3-4).

All these years later, like the Magi, we can still find our way by looking at the stars.

Advent Actions

1. Take time this Advent to do a little stargazing. Many of us live within the confines of the city, where it's difficult to see the constellations in all their fullness. You may need to drive out of the city, where there are no street lights, to get the real effect of nature's starry sky.

First, familiarize yourself with some of the constellations like the Orion Constellation, which can be seen only in the winter. It disappears from the rays of the sun in the fall. Within the Orion Constellation is the M42 Nebula, a nursery where new stars are born.

Second, watch the You-Tube video, "See the Constellations." This video will tell you how to identify the Orion constellation. (Find the link at www.faithlab.com/advent.)

2. Watch the You-Tube video "The Hubble Deep Field: The Most Important Image Ever Taken." (Find the link at www.faithlab.com/advent.) This video gives a very good understanding of the vastness of God's universe. Take some time to reflect on how small the world is in relation to the universe God has created. Even so, the Bible still says that God knows each of us to the point that the very hairs of our heads are numbered (Matthew 10:30).

3. If you really want to have an unforgettable experience of God's world of outer space, find someone with a nice telescope who can locate some of the more familiar constellations. Take a child with you to view them on a clear, starry night. Take some hot chocolate along. Watch the magic in the child's eyes as he or she sees part of God's world come into focus in an entirely new way.

Prayer

God of the Heavens and the Earth,

We acknowledge that we are earthbound. We have our minds and our hearts attached to the earth. We don't give much attention to what goes on above us, unless it's a thundercloud or some other form of bad weather that interferes with our daily lives. We don't take the time to marvel at the constellations.

God of Heaven and Earth, if we would look up, would You send us a light that would show us the way? If we would look up to You, would You send us a light that would illuminate our meetings, conversations, decisions, and relationships? Might we hear a voice that would send us on different paths?

We are earthbound, Lord, but You are not. Through Jesus, You sent us Your Holy Spirit. We thank You that while our physical residence is still here, we can claim a home in heaven as promised through Your son Jesus.

Through us, show others Your power and Your strength that we might show others the way to a heavenly home. Through Your physical world, remind us of Your majesty, the vastness of Your creation, and Your ongoing attention to the details of humanity.

We continue to marvel at your greatness, Lord. We join with the Psalmist who wrote: "When I consider your heavens, the work of your fingers, the moon and the stars, which you have set in place, what is man that you are mindful of him, the son of man that you care for him?" (Psalm 8:3-4).

Thank You for loving us in such a loving and personal way. Amen.

Pondering the Significance of the Virgin Birth
December 7

*S*ome have called the story a myth—the story of Mary with child, conceived while she was still a virgin. Calling this story a myth is the only alternative you and I have, should we not hold a fancy for a virgin birth.

If this story is a myth, then what really happened? The only other logical answer is that Jesus would have been born out of wedlock with Joseph as the likely father. The virgin birth story would have been created by the early church to cover up Mary and Joseph's sin and to promote a lie that Jesus was divine.

The early church? Yes. Who would have believed such a story, after all, in Joseph and Mary's day? Certainly, no one who knew Mary and Joseph. Can't you see Joseph trying to convince friends that Mary was still a virgin?

"Yeah, Mary's pregnant. But I'm not the real father. Now, don't get the wrong idea. Mary hasn't been sleeping around or anything. She's not that kind of girl. Then who's the father? Well, that's a good question. What are you guys laughing about? Okay, I admit, it does sound hard to believe, but it's the truth, I tell you. The Holy Spirit came upon her, and she conceived."

This is the biblical position: Mary was a virgin. She conceived the baby through a miraculous intervention of God. Either you believe the Bible or you don't.

The virgin birth has never been an issue for me. Here's why.

I believe that God created the heavens and the earth, "ex nihilo," out of nothing. So for me, other miracles are sort of downhill from there. I suppose those same people who have a problem with the virgin birth, also have a problem believing God created the world. That may put me in the "simple faith" crowd, but Jesus did say that unless we have the faith of a child we cannot enter the kingdom of God.

Mary knew the truth. Joseph knew the truth. Mary's cousin Elizabeth knew the truth. That was enough. I doubt they spent much time trying to convince friends and relatives about visits from angels bearing such news, although people of that day may have been more receptive to that sort of thing than those of us in the twenty-first century.

This, I do know. You do not read about Jesus' virgin birth any more in the New Testament after the birth narratives. It's not a point Jesus stressed at all in His teachings. Paul doesn't mention it, but it is an aspect of our Christian faith that we should embrace.

Either we embrace it as truth or we believe it as myth; a myth that would have arisen during the years that followed the deaths of Joseph, Mary and Jesus to substantiate that Jesus was from God and therefore, divine. Other than clearing Mary and Joseph of any wrongdoing, the only reason to make up such a story is to substantiate that from the beginning of His life, Jesus was divine.

Had Jesus been conceived as you and I were, it would not have taken away from the type of life He lived. However, it would have taken away the Apostle John's claim that Jesus lived before the creation of the world, that everything that was made was made through Him (John 1:10).

It would take away the claim of Jesus' first cousin, John the Baptist, six months his elder, who said: "This was he of whom I said, 'He who comes after me has surpassed me because he was before me'" (John 1:15).

It would take away the claims of Jesus himself, who said

before his ascension into heaven that he "came from the Father and entered the world; now I am leaving the world and going back to the Father" (John 16:28) and on another occasion when he said: "I and the Father are one" (John 10:30).

So, you see, if we set the virgin birth of Jesus up as a myth, then we have started a domino effect that negates the words of John the Apostle, the words of John the Baptist, and the words of Jesus Himself.

You must believe either that Jesus was CREATED as you and I were, or that Jesus was BEGOTTEN, as it says in the KJV of John 3:16.

If Jesus was created, then He came into this world no different from you or me. If Jesus was created, then whatever Jesus did while on this earth could not have had any eternal difference on our souls. Though he may have blazed a trail on earth through His teachings for us to follow, it would have been impossible for Him to blaze a trail to heaven for us to follow.

If Jesus was created, then Advent is meaningless because Jesus came to us as a baby in Bethlehem through the same birthing channels as any other human being. Advent would only be a time to remember a man who came and lived a unique life, rather than a Savior who has the power and authority to save us from our sins.

Consider John's gospel when it says: "The Word became flesh and made his dwelling among us" (John 1:14). Another translation says that the Lord "tabernacled" among us or "pitched his tent" among us.

The fact that the Lord pitched His tent among us, brings great peace to our lives. We can find peace because through Christ we have a mediator, One who is able to represent us before God. Jesus qualifies as our mediator because He has walked in our shoes. Jesus understands the trappings of humanity because He has been where we are.

Paul said: "For there is one God, and one mediator also between God and men, the man Christ Jesus" (1 Timothy 2:5). We can have peace because Jesus is able to understand our problems. Hebrews 2:17-18 says:

> *And it was necessary for Jesus to be like us, his brothers, so that he could be our merciful and faithful High Priest before God, a Priest who would be both merciful to us and faithful to God in dealing with the sins of the people. For since he himself has now been through suffering and temptation, he knows what it is like when we suffer and are tempted, and he is wonderfully able to help us (TLB).*

Perhaps you've heard the saying, "Never judge someone until you've walked a mile in his shoes." Well, these verses from Hebrews tell us that Jesus has walked a mile, and then some, in our shoes.

Christmas began with the miracle of the virgin birth. Each new believer is another birth into God's kingdom and introduces people to one of the world's most awesome realities, that the God who spoke and created the heavens and the earth knows each of us, is prepared to forgive us of sin and provide guidance for our lives through the Holy Spirit, with the promise of eternal life through Christ our Lord.

During Advent, each of us should spend some time pondering the significance of the virgin birth. If it were myth, we'd have no reason to sing "Joy to the World, the Lord Is Come." But since Jesus was born of a virgin, we can sing, "Heaven came down and glory filled my soul."

This Advent season give God thanks for the virgin birth of Jesus. Because Jesus came from heaven to help us deal with life, we have confidence that through His Holy Spirit, we can find our way.

Advent Actions

1. Apologetics involves defending or proving the truth of Christian doctrines. This devotional was apologetic in nature. Outline the key points this devotional used to defend the virgin birth of Jesus.

2. What other points would you add?

3. After you outline the key points, review the key reasons the devotional made regarding why the virgin birth is a necessary component of the Christian faith.

4. It's possible during Advent for God to give you an opportunity to discuss the virgin birth with a skeptic. Ask the person if he or she believes in the virgin birth. If not, "Why not?" After listening, ask if you can share why you believe the virgin birth is a vital part of the Christian faith, and why you believe it to be true.

5. Review the Apostles' Creed. Note the inclusion of the virgin birth.

> *I believe in God, the Father Almighty,*
> *the Maker of heaven and earth*
> *and in Jesus Christ, His only Son, our Lord:*
> *Who was conceived by the Holy Ghost,*
> *born of the Virgin Mary,*
> *suffered under Pontius Pilate,*
> *was crucified, dead, and buried;*
> *He descended into hell.*
> *The third day He arose again from the dead;*

He ascended into heaven,
and sitteth on the right hand of God the Father
    Almighty
from thence he shall come to judge the quick and the
    dead.
I believe in the Holy Ghost;
the holy catholic church;
the communion of saints;
the forgiveness of sins;
the resurrection of the body;
and the life everlasting.
Amen.[6]

Prayer

Incarnate God,

We are in awe that You became so vulnerable in order to show us Your love. Occasionally, we become vulnerable to show people our love, but we are very cautious. When we show love, we usually like to have an "out" in case something goes wrong. In case we are misunderstood, we like to have a quick exit plan.

You became one of us. You were God, yes, but You took on the skin, the emotions, the temptations, the confining arrangements of our environment, and You lived among us. Consequently, we know You understand us. You've walked in our shoes, except You never gave in to Your temptations.

You were fully human, yet You demonstrated the God side of your incarnation and defeated sin. You crushed Satan. You even defeated death, our last enemy. Had You not pitched Your tent among us, Lord, we would not understand peace to the depth that we know it. Our fears of the grave would hold power over us. Death cannot have the last word now, Lord, because Jesus, born of the Virgin Mary, defeated death. We praise You, forever and ever. Amen.

Peace That Runs Deep
December 8

Back in the 1970s, one of the hit songs by the Eagles was "Peaceful Easy Feeling." The Eagles are one of my favorite rock and roll bands. However, I must admit, when I began paying close attention to some of the lyrics, many of their songs that are imbued with happiness and peace are lacking in substance. Instead they promote acts of self-gratification.

In the song, "Peaceful Easy Feeling," the Eagles sing about a man who wants to sleep with a brown-skinned woman in the desert beneath a billion stars because he believes it will give him a peaceful, easy feeling.

Not much has changed since the 1970s or since the days of Adam and Eve, for that matter. Most people are looking to fulfill their wants and desires with acts of the flesh. People are looking for a peaceful, easy feeling that won't let them down.

The world teaches that peace comes initially through one of our five senses. We are taught that if something feels good to the body, it must be good for the soul. This was the ancient philosophy of the Epicureans. If you listen, you can hear this philosophy in the lyrics of many secular songs. You will see it posted on billboards, shown on television, or at the movie theater.

What people really want is a peace with depth, but too often they settle for that which gratifies the body. Any peaceful, easy feeling that comes through our senses will eventually let us down.

This kind of superficial peace is like spraying water on the leaves of a thirsty plant. If the plant could speak, it might tell us that the water feels good to its dried leaves. But unless that plant gets water down to its roots, a little mist on the leaves will do little or nothing to help it survive.

Unless you and I allow the Living Water of Jesus to seep down to the roots of our souls, we will forever be chasing rainbows.

I'm always a bit amused at the Easter and Christmas crowds—those people who show up a couple of times a year in church to get a little religion. They are looking for a peaceful, easy feeling, not much more. They want a little Jesus sprinkled on them so that they can feel good, but the Water rarely seeps down to the roots of their souls. They don't allow it. They leave the service unchanged. With a religious sprinkling that they hope will create that peaceful, easy feeling, they leave church until the next holy season.

In our society today, the peaceful easy feeling is pursued mostly through people's senses. People must seek repetitive occurrences of pleasurable moments to find any peace because once the pleasure is gone, so is the peace. Self-gratification becomes a god. It's a trap. The more the acts are repeated, the more in bondage people become.

In opposition to self-gratification, the Bible teaches that lasting peace comes from having the Lord near. Among other ways, God's presence is felt through prayer, the Holy Spirit, and Holy Scripture.

Prayer

In November of 2006, Benedict XVI told a group of young people gathered at Vatican City that: "Genuine prayer transforms hearts, opens us to dialogue, understanding and reconciliation, and breaks down the walls erected by violence, hatred and revenge."[7]

If we pray with the intent of prayer changing others or

changing circumstances, we have missed the greatest benefit of praying. The greatest benefit of prayer is how prayer changes the one who
prays. Prayer brings us into the presence of God. The more we stay
in the presence of God and understand the nature of God, the more
opportunity we have of becoming the person God wants us to be.

Jesus said: "A student is not above his teacher, but everyone
who is fully trained will be like his teacher" (Luke 6:40). Our goal is
to be like Jesus. We can't become like Jesus without spending time
with Him in prayer. A byproduct of spending time with Jesus is
peace.

Paul was very clear about the source of peace in his letter to
the church at Philippi:

> Do not be anxious about anything, but in everything,
> by prayer and petition, with thanksgiving, present
> your requests to God. And the peace of God, which
> transcends all understanding, will guard your hearts
> and your minds in Christ Jesus (Philippians 4:6-7).

Holy Spirit

Because the Lord's presence is mediated through his Holy
Spirit, we can have a peace that's deep enough to sustain us, even in
the most difficult times of life.

Oceanographers say the sea remains tranquil below twenty-five feet, regardless of how badly the storm rages on the surface.
Storms will come in this life. Storms are not respecters of persons.
During the storms of life, we discover that self-gratification is about
as deep as a puddle. In a storm, self-gratification is as useless as a
bathing suit at the North Pole.

Without a peace that runs deep, we become overrun with
our anxieties. We may sink beneath the waves, never to return.
The Lord wants our peace to be deeply rooted, long lasting, and
dependent upon His presence, rather than upon circumstances.

God said to Joshua: "As I was with Moses, so I will be with you; I will never leave you nor forsake you" (Joshua 1:5). Joshua had witnessed the good, the bad, and the ugly of the Hebrew nation. He knew that the nation could not have survived a forty-year wilderness experience without God's presence. He knew he could not survive as the nation's leader if God did not provide for him the same presence that He provided for Moses. God's promise gave Joshua the peace he needed.

Jesus' talk about leaving created great anxiety among His disciples. He needed to provide them with peaceful assurances that His presence would always be felt. He said to His disciples: "And surely I am with you always, to the very end of the age" (Matthew 28:20).

Jesus made His presence possible to them and to us through His gift of the Holy Spirit. As Jesus prepared to leave His disciples, He said:

> All this I have spoken while still with you. But the Counselor, the Holy Spirit, whom the Father will send in my name, will teach you all things and will remind you of everything I have said to you. Peace I leave with you; my peace I give you. I do not give to you as the world gives. Do not let your hearts be troubled and do not be afraid (John 14:25-27).

The presence of Christ in our lives does not protect us from grief or tragedy. The presence of Christ does allow us to find our way in the midst of them. When life brings circumstances that threaten to rob us of peace, Jesus is our guarantee that they do not have the final word.

Holy Scripture

God's Word is a constant source of peace for us. In God's

Word we find many treasures to help us find our way when our peace is threatened. For example, our own bent to sin is a major threat to rob us of our peace. From God's Word we learn that sin doesn't have to have the final word in our lives either. While consequences of sin may linger, peace in our hearts is possible. "If we confess our sins, he is faithful and just and will forgive us our sins and purify us from all unrighteousness" (1 John 1:9). This verse brings peace because it helps us know that we can get right with the Lord.

Other verses remind us of the value of staying away from sin altogether. Isaiah said: "Those who walk uprightly enter into peace" (Isaiah 57:2). The Psalmist who wrote the first Psalm understood this. Peace was no doubt part of the blessings he spoke of when he wrote:

> *Blessed is the man who does not walk in the counsel of the wicked or stand in the way of sinners or sit in the seat of mockers. But his delight is in the law of the LORD, and on his law he meditates day and night. He is like a tree planted by streams of water, which yields its fruit in season and whose leaf does not wither. Whatever he does prospers (Psalm 1:1-3).*

Peace runs deep when we run our roots deep into God's word. God's word helps us find our way. When we know God's will and the promises of scripture, we can make choices and have assurances that keep us from becoming chaff blown away by the wind (v. 4).

For example, knowing that God is watching over us as we seek to walk in righteous ways (v. 6) brings added peace. It doesn't mean that bad things never happen to good people. It does mean that God will not forsake us if they do.

Throughout this Advent season, peace is possible because Christ is with us. The promise God made to Joshua and the promise that Jesus made to His disciples are the same promises the Lord God makes to us. Because "Jesus Christ is the same yesterday and today and forever" (Hebrews 13:8), we can count on these promises and count on the peace that Jesus brings through his Holy Spirit and through his Holy Word.

Since "all Scripture is God-breathed and is useful for teaching, rebuking, correcting and training in righteousness, so that the man of God may be thoroughly equipped for every good work" (2 Timothy 3:16-17), a steady diet of scripture reading helps us chart our path and find our way. We cannot have peace if we lose our way. We cannot find our way on our own. We need guidance, and God has provided guidance through His Word.

Righteousness lived out from the knowledge we gain from Holy Scripture can provide us with peace and help us know the Prince of Peace, the One Advent is all about.

Advent Actions

1. Watch a video of an Eagles performance of "Peaceful Easy Feeling." (See www.faithlab.com/advent.) As you listen to the lyrics, think about those things that bring you a peaceful easy feeling. As you think about them, ask yourself, "Are the things this group sings about things that last or things that are temporary?" More importantly, determine if these things are moral or sinful. Do they harm your body or your spirit? Do they lead you toward God or away from God? Think again about the Eagles' song, "Peaceful Easy Feeling." Are all peaceful easy feelings a result of things that are good for us? What about the things the Eagles sing about?

2. Memorize one of these verses of scripture about peace or post the verse somewhere prominent during the remainder of the Advent season.

> "Listen to what God the Lord will say; he promises peace to his people" (Psalm 85:8).
> "The mind of sinful man is death, but the mind controlled by the Spirit is life and peace" (Romans 8:6).
> "A heart at peace gives life to the body, but envy rots the bones" (Proverbs 14:30).

3. Keep a prayer journal through Advent. Jot down simple prayers. Meditate on Philippians 4:7:

> Do not be anxious about anything, but in everything, by prayer and petition, with thanksgiving, present your requests to God. And the peace of God, which

*transcends all understanding, will guard your hearts
and your minds in Christ Jesus.*

4. Sit quietly and ask yourself, "What am I anxious about?" Once you've identified your anxieties, talk to the Lord about them. Do what Paul says: "by prayer and petition, with thanksgiving, present your requests to God" (Philemon 4:6b). Peace will follow.

Prayer

God of Peace,

We fret over more than we should. We wring our hands and worry because we haven't learned to bring our anxieties to You. As is often prayed in twelve-step programs: "grant us the serenity to accept the things that cannot be changed, the courage to change the things that we can, and the wisdom to distinguish the one from the other" (Reinhold Niebuhr).

What we all want, God, is peace. We want peace from the onslaught of a world that never ceases its advance of disease, aging and decay. We feel like Adam, who was forced to compete with the thorns to raise a crop after he and Eve were cast from the garden. It's hard to get ahead in this world, Lord.

Much of our lack of peace is our own undoing, Lord. We are our own worst enemy. We fail over and over to carry out Your commands, which You have laid out as a path for us to follow, a path that would produce the most peace in our lives. Help us find our way by showing us where we are not following You, and we shall begin to make a new start. As we do, give us that peaceful feeling, one that we know comes from walking with You. Amen.

What God Wants for Christmas
December 9

There are still gifts to buy, meals to cook, and trips to take as we move through the Advent season. If we are not careful, we will become so busy we will miss the person that's standing between us and Christmas, a man who's pointing us in the direction we need to go: John the Baptist.

How can you miss John the Baptist? There he is standing in the middle of the Jordan River, speaking in a loud, commanding voice. He's a bit on the eccentric side. He looks like a weird character you might see on the streets of San Francisco.

He looks a little bit like a cave man standing there in his garment of camel's hair. He's been living in the desert. I bet he has body odor. After all, how many baths can you take in the desert?

He's a rough, tough-looking guy. He eats what the desert lets him eat: locusts and wild honey. I bet he has bad breath. And yet, there on the edge of the wilderness, people come out of the villages to hear this man preach. Before you can get to Christmas, you need to hear the message of John the Baptist.

John's entire purpose is to get us ready for the coming of Jesus. He fulfilled the words of Isaiah the prophet, who said that God would send His messenger. His voice would be a voice crying out in the wilderness: "Prepare the way of the Lord, make his paths straight" (Mark 1:3b).

This was John's role, and he fulfilled it by preaching a

baptism of repentance for the forgiveness of sins. The gospel writer, Mark, paints a picture of people coming from the countryside and the villages and entering the water of the Jordan River, confessing their sins as John baptized them.

What a scene that must have been—a stinking man who needed a bath, dressed in camel hair, and dipping people in the Jordan. The line was long. They didn't even have to sing thirty verses of "Just as I Am."

You can't smell John's body odor or his halitosis. You can't feel the trickling of the Jordan running through your legs or the rocks from the bottom pressing against your feet. But I pray that you can hear John's message because his message still stands between us and Christmas Day. He bellows it from the pages of Holy Scripture. We need to repent of our sins!

I once read of a man with a nagging secret that he couldn't keep any longer. In the confessional he admitted that for years he had been stealing building supplies from the lumberyard where he worked. "What did you take?" his parish priest asked. "Enough to build my own home and enough for my son's house. And houses for our two daughters. And our cottage at the lake."

"This is very serious," the priest said, "I shall have to think of a far-reaching penance. Have you ever done a retreat?" "No, Father, I haven't," the man replied. "But if you can get the plans, I can get the lumber."

This man came to the priest to admit his guilt, but he didn't come with much desire to change his habits, did he? Giving this kind of confession to God is like giving a kid a battery-operated toy with no batteries. It looks good but it has no power. Admitting guilt may look good, but without repentance, confession has no power. Repentance happens when we turn away from our sin and move toward God.

As you've moved down your list of gifts to buy or make for

others, have you thought much about what you might give to the Lord this Christmas? After all, He was the first recipient of gifts during this time of the year. Why should we leave Him out? It's His birthday.

Perhaps the Great High Priest would like to receive our confessions. But believe me; the Lord knows whether or not our confessions are coupled with a sincere desire to make changes. Repentance is the batteries in our confessions. Repentance is the power that makes our confessions mean something.

John the Baptist came preaching a baptism of repentance for the forgiveness of sins. We must immerse ourselves in the waters of repentance as we confess our sins. Otherwise, we've done nothing more than wrap a piece of coal in pretty wrapping and presented it to Jesus as His gift.

Do you want to give the Lord something for Christmas? Then begin with the one issue that weighs the most upon your conscience and admit it to the Lord as sin. God already knows about it. What God desires is that we name it and then turn away from it. Pray to God for the discipline and strength to make the changes you need in your life. Know that the Lord will keep His promise to forgive your sins and cleanse you from all unrighteousness.

John the Baptist may have had body odor. He may have had halitosis. However, he didn't smell as bad as those who try to fool the Lord and others with an occasional token of religious activity that seems to pop up during the holidays. The fact that we come down to the waters to hear John the Baptist preach doesn't mean we are willing to get wet. However, the fact that you are reading this book of Advent devotionals indicates that you are on a spiritual quest. You are obviously being intentional about preparing for the arrival of Christmas.

So, go ahead. Take that next step. Many of us can admit we are wrong about certain things, but how many of us are willing to change? The Lord would like nothing better for Christmas than to receive our confessions and then help us find a different or better way to live our lives. Confession and repentance yield peace.

Advent Actions

1. Unless you change one thing about your Christian walk with Christ during Advent, and walk into the New Year having repented of an old way of doing things, you may not have given Jesus what He wants most for Christmas.

2. "What about the food I give to the food bank? What about the angel I pull from the angel tree at the church that goes for an underprivileged child? What about the Christmas caroling we did at the retirement home?" You want to know if those counted as gifts for Jesus? Here's my question: "Were you motivated to do those out of love, or did you do them to keep from feeling guilty?" If you have to ask the question, it makes me wonder. Obviously, any time we do something out of love for others, it's a gift to Jesus. Remember, Jesus said, "Whatsoever you do for the least of these brothers of mine, you do so unto me" (Matthew 25:45).

3. The key question here is: "What does Jesus want for Christmas?" Isn't that what we ask of everyone else that we love? So, why not Jesus? I contend that in addition to wanting us to help "the least of these," Jesus wants the same thing that John the Baptist said Jesus wanted so long ago, "repentance."

If Advent is really going to be about Jesus, then at some point we must take inventory. We must allow Jesus to point out where we are not measuring up. We must see our sin and decide to turn from it and do life differently, and not just differently, but the way Jesus has asked us to do it. The payoff is peace.

Prayer

God Who Convicts and Forgives,

We are people who get into ruts and routines. We sit in the same pew in church. We eat the same foods. We get up and go to bed at the same times. We eat at the same restaurants. We hang out with the same friends. We hold on to the same sins. Our sin becomes like an old blanket. It's almost comforting. Yet, afterwards we hate ourselves and wish we were different. Even so, we can't find the discipline to change—at least we haven't found the discipline. Can You help us change that? I know that's a dumb question, Lord.

The power of the resurrection is available to us. You spoke, and the world came into being. The angel Gabriel told Mary that nothing is impossible with You. So helping us find the power to turn away from our sin is nothing for You. We know that we must be committed and truly want to make a break from our sin and follow You.

So now, Lord, we confess our sin. We lay it before You. Our gift to You this Advent is our repentance. We lay our sins before You and turn from them, but we do not do so in our own strength. We ask for Your help and ask that You give us the power to overcome the temptation to return to our sin. Amen.

Life Is Like a Field Trial
December 10

"Yelp! Yelp! Yelp!" The trainer barks out signals and blows his whistle occasionally as Jake, a three-year-old bird dog, zigzags his way through the thickets in search of quail. Jake covers a swath of territory several hundred yards wide, staying within a ten o'clock to two o'clock radius. His white, lean body flashes through the oaks, underbrush, and blooming dogwoods. His owner is perched on his favorite horse and leads a gallery of about sixty other riders who have come to the field trial in Thomasville, Georgia to enjoy some of the pleasures of Southern living: woods, dogs, quail, horses, fresh air, and the gathering of people who share such passions.

As Jake works the thickets, a judge follows closely on horseback. He watches with the eyes of an expert and knows whether Jake and his owner are in sync. The dog has amazing instincts, but is prone to veer off the course without the constant instructions of his master. Jake has the ability to catch the scent of quail, birds so well camouflaged that unless they run or fly, a human would walk right past them and never see them.

After several minutes of sprints, the scent of the birds brings Jake to an abrupt halt. His tail stands up straight like the flag on a mailbox as he signals his find. His owner dismounts his horse, pulls his single-shot, 20-gauge shotgun from its sleeve and walks toward his dog. Jake holds his point like a statue. More than anything, the dog wants praise from his master. Before it comes, he must hold his position and birds must be flushed to prove that Jake's nose really knows.

His owner kicks the brush. He makes one pass, then another. Suddenly, the covey releases its position and scatters to another location. The gun is discharged. It's nothing more than a victory shot. The blank 20-gauge shell propels milo seed into the air that falls to the earth to be eaten later by the birds. Jake's owner collars his dog, praises him for his work, and gives him water from a jug. Then Jake is released, off to find more birds.

"Yelp! Yelp! Yelp!" The choreography between master and dog continues. Far out in front of the gallery of horses and riders, Jake streaks through the brush. Much of the time he's out of sight, but the judge maintains a close distance at all times. If Jake flushes a covey without pointing, the judge knows. If he fails to respond to the voice of his master, the judge knows. If he points to a covey and no birds are found, the judge knows.

The gallery soon learns that they are out of position to judge most of the action. Most people in the gallery don't have the critical eye of the judge, either. But there are times the entire gallery knows when a dog has misbehaved or has been mistaken.

Sometimes the dog becomes so oblivious to its master's voice that a scout has to retrieve the animal. When it happens too often, the dog is removed from the course. It doesn't take a field trial expert to know the dog hasn't done well.

The gallery also gets to witness the dog's many successes. Jake's master raises his hat to indicate a possible find. The other riders surround the area as the dog holds his point. The gallery appreciates the dog's God-given instincts and the skill of the trainer, who helps him get the most out of what the dog's been given. Even so, only the judge is close enough and skilled enough to pass judgment on the animal's success or failure—whether he makes the grade or whether he doesn't.

You and I are part of a gallery through a lot of life's events. We may know some details of a particular situation, and we may have seen some things with our own eyes—sometimes good, sometimes bad. But rarely are we close enough to see it all. We cannot judge what we cannot see. Even when we are in a position to see it all, we must remember we are not infallible in our verdicts.

There is only one Infallible Judge close enough to every situation to decide who is in the right and who is in the wrong. As members of the gallery, we must be careful not to try to take the place of the Judge. We are not the final authority.

John, the writer of Revelation, pictures the only Infallible Judge like this: "I saw heaven standing open and there before me was a white horse, whose rider is called Faithful and True. With justice he judges and makes war" (Revelation 19:11).

We cannot see or know all the good or bad in any situation. But the rider on the white horse in heaven is in such a position. Nothing we do escapes His eyes. If we focus on the course others are running without giving eye to our own, we may fail to notice how well we are running our own race, or how poorly.

Jesus once said:

> Do not judge, or you too will be judged. For in the same way you judge others, you will be judged, and with the measure you use, it will be measured to you. Why do you look at the speck of sawdust in your brother's eye and pay no attention to the plank in your own eye? How can you say to your brother, 'Let me take the speck out of your eye,' when all the time there is a plank in your own eye? You hypocrite, first take the plank out of your own eye, and then you will see clearly to remove the speck from your brother's eye (Matthew 7:1-5).

During Advent, our lives are usually cast together with the

lives of family and friends. Many times these are family and friends
we don't get to see very often. Some of these gatherings are pleasant, and some of them are filled with tension and stress. We may
be tempted to judge family and others whom we have not seen in a
while, by the way they look, how they raise their kids, the way they
spend their money, and what they choose to value in life.

It's a great temptation to pronounce judgment on them at
some point during the holidays, making the meeting unpleasant.
The Christmas joy is quickly glossed over with Christmas jousting.

A much better way to spend our time with family and friends
is to look for opportunities to give a positive witness for our Lord.
God cannot be pleased with us if we become too busy being the family judge, pronouncing our verdicts on everyone.

This is not to say there is not a place to talk about faith with
family or friends. It's Jesus' birthday after all. Talking about issues
of faith during the celebration of the Lord's birthday seems natural
to many Christians. However, there is a difference between judging
others and giving a word of witness about one's faith in the Lord.
While one lifts up Jesus, the other preaches down to others, and
gatherings with family at Christmas may not be the time for that.

It's difficult to minister to those within one's own family, especially to those we see only once or twice a year. Jesus' first message
to family and friends in the synagogue in Nazareth was a message of
good news taken from the scroll of Isaiah:

> *The Spirit of the Lord is on me, because he has anoint-*
> *ed me to preach good news to the poor. He has sent me*
> *to proclaim freedom for the prisoners and recovery of*
> *sight for the blind, to release the oppressed, to proclaim*
> *the year of the Lord's favor (Luke 4:18-19).*

This part of His message was received well. However, the
next part of Jesus' message got Him in trouble. He began to compare

His own family and neighbors to the people who lived in the days of Elijah and Elisha, the prophets. God did not send Elijah to his own people, but to a widow in Zarephath. God's prophet Elisha didn't heal any lepers in Israel, but only those in Syria. Those who heard Jesus read between the lines took his words as an insult. They judged Him on the spot and sought to kill Him, which actually proved Jesus' words. They took Him to the brow of a hill in town, where they intended to push him over the edge, but He escaped through the crowd.

There will be a lot of yelping around the dinner tables and within family circles during the holidays. It usually happens when the family gathers and disagreeable subjects arise or old wounds are opened. Make sure when you are making your points that they are done in love, and not seen by others as self-righteous judgment or mean-spirited banter. When you feel you must fire off, make sure that you aren't shooting to kill. Make sure your shots rain down like harmless seeds of faith, which others around can come back to at a later time and gather for nourishment.

We may feel like sheep among wolves, even among family and friends sometimes, but as Jesus said, we must be "as shrewd as snakes and as innocent as doves" (Matthew 10:16). This is how we help others find their way and maintain peace within the family during Advent and Christmas.

Advent Actions

1. Begin a tradition or continue a tradition during Advent. In the story, "Life is Like a Field Trial," the dogs and the trainer had a kind of choreography going, each knowing the movements of the other from previous hunts. Traditions are like that—they give us a kind of comfort and familiarity that bring some continuity to life. When events come only once a year, traditions help bridge the gap from one year to the next, and help us form lasting memories.

To learn more online about the Advent Wreath, the Jesse Tree, and the Good Deeds Manger as ideas for Advent traditions. (Visit www.faithlab.com/advent for links.)

2. Work very hard to maintain a spirit of unity and fairness in bringing together the traditions of multiple families during the holidays. As families age and grow, traditions grow and change. This becomes difficult for some people to understand and accept. Sometimes young people are put under undue pressure to be in certain places at certain times, as if their love for the family is being tested by their presence. Most families who love each other want to be together during the holidays. However, it's impossible to be in two places at one time. When people in your family are put in a no-win situation, show the depth of your love by being understanding, even if you are disappointed.

3. Blended families have unique challenges and pressures during the holidays to meet everyone's demands and expectations. Dr. Berna Skrypnek, who specializes in child-parent relationships, says that the holidays will be the most enjoyable and meaningful for blended

families when "each side brings well-established traditions to the mix and every child past toddlerhood has bought into these rituals. Pulling two families together means honoring traditions from each side and creating new ones that reflect the new identity of the blended family, balancing the past and future."[8] She also says that it's important to keep the extended family involved during the holidays. At some point, grandparents, aunts and uncles need to be involved during the holidays, Skrypnek says. "Ex-spouses need to work in a collaborative fashion to reduce stress for kids ahead of time. A little bit of thoughtfulness can minimize the discomfort and maximize the comfort."[9]

Prayer

God Who Loves the Family,

It's amazing that you chose to enter into this world and become a part of a family. For all of the good that there is within families, there isn't one of our families that doesn't have some quirks. Some of them have more than a few.

At some point during Advent, You know we will have to share time with family whether we want to or not, Lord. This is the time of the year, like none other, that we are reminded we are all a part of a family unit. While we think of having to put up with other members of the family during this time of the year, we don't usually pause to think that others in the family might be thinking the same thing about us. We, after all, look at ourselves as having it all together, having minor issues compared to others in the family. It's so easy to judge, Lord, and so difficult to love and to accept.

Through the story of the field trial You have reminded us that there is only one Infallible Judge. Forgive us for trying to claim Your seat. Instead, help us to be more like You: accepting, loving, kind and gracious. This Advent, help us to practice grace and love on members of our own family. Help us to listen more and practice hospitality towards even the most difficult members of our family, including ourselves. Amen.

The Most Important Thing About a Name
December 11

When God was handing out common sense, some people didn't get in line. In 2002, a Turkish couple living in Germany tried to name their baby Osama bin Laden. They stated that Osama was a good man for his people and for their culture. Their request was denied by the German government, which has laws that make harmful or dishonorable names illegal. That sounds like governmental common sense, which is an oxymoron, I think.

It's difficult to imagine how those parents could have such a warped world view that they thought Osama bin Laden was a good name for their child. It would be less surprising if the couple had never traveled outside their Turkish village, having had no access to outside worldviews or opinions. But these people are living in Germany! Then again, Germany is the country that produced Adolf Hitler. I hope his name is on the country's list of dishonorable names.

I'd be surprised if any parents in America need to be told not to name their son Osama or Adolf. However, common sense does tell most people to give each of their children different names. I'm not sure where George Foreman was standing when common sense was handed out.

George is a very likeable guy. I think he's even an ordained minister. I suppose he really likes his name because he named his children George Foreman, Jr., Freeda George, Georgetta, George III, George IV, George V and George VI. I guess it makes it easy to call all of them to the dinner table. When he cooks for them, on his George Foreman grill, no doubt, all he has to do is yell, "Hey, all you Georges, come eat!" With that many children, that really makes a lot of sense when you stop to think about it.

I've often wondered how much of children's personalities come from their names. Some children have a great burden to carry into adulthood having so much or so little expected of them because of their names. Sometimes a name is empowering, allowing a person to grow into a self-understanding that is positive and filled with self-esteem.

We see examples of this in the Bible. It's interesting that so many of the characters' personalities fit their names perfectly. Or is it that their names fit their personalities? For example, Adam means "human being" and Eve means "life giving." Abraham means "father of multitudes." Three of the world's most important religions trace their heritage to Abraham: Christianity, Judaism, and Islam.

Jacob, who tricked his brother out of his birthright and his inheritance, means "trickster," and it was changed to "Israel," which means "he strives with God." This name change occurred the night he wrestled "with God," or "an angel of God."

Moses means "drawn out." Not only was he drawn out of the water as a baby, but God drew him out of the desert as a shepherd to use him to draw out a nation of people from Pharaoh's bondage. Achan means "troubler." In Israel's military campaign in Canaan, his theft of items in the destruction of Jericho led to a defeat in their next battle. His actions troubled the nation.

Ruth means "companion/friend." When her husband and father-in-law died, she refused to leave Naomi, her mother-in-law. David means "beloved." This great king was Israel's most beloved king, who was a direct ancestor of Jesus. Jesus, the name above all names, means "Yahweh is salvation."

Sometimes in the Bible, children had to endure the burden

of their names. When the Ark of the Covenant was captured by the Philistines, Hophni and Phinehas, the sons of Eli, were killed. When the wife of Phinehas heard the news, she went into premature labor and gave birth. She had a difficult delivery. As she was dying she named her boy Ichabod, which means "the glory has departed from Israel." Imagine having to carry the burden of that name.

The prophet Hosea demonstrated that even millenniums ago preachers used their kids as sermon illustrations. He named one child Lo-Ruhamah, because God was no longer going to show love to the people of Israel. He named another one Lo-Ammi, meaning God was no longer going to be their God, and they were not going to be his people because of their unfaithfulness. The names of Hosea's children reminded Israel that they were being judged by God.

What kind of name has been given to you? Perhaps you've been given a name that made your life easier than it might otherwise have been. Perhaps your life has been more difficult because of the name given to you, like the boy from Shel Silverstein's humorous song, "A Boy Named Sue."

With his gravelly voice, Johnny Cash sings of the day Sue met his real dad, a man who named him and left him at birth. Years of pent up anger exploded when the two finally met as adults, and the son began to fight the old man, demanding an explanation for giving him such a name. And he said:

> Son, this world is rough
> And if a man's gonna make it, he's gotta be tough
> And I knew I wouldn't be there to help ya along.
> So I give ya that name and I said good-bye
> I knew you'd have to get tough or die
> And it's that name that helped to make you strong.

The song ends with these words:

> I got all choked up and I threw down my gun

And I called him my pa, and he called me his son,
And I come away with a different point of view.
And I think about him, now and then,
Every time I try and every time I win,
And if I ever have a son, I think I'm gonna name him
Bill or George! Anything but Sue!
I still hate that name! [10]

But whether our names are difficult or easy, each of us will be judged based on whether our name is written in the Lamb's Book of Life. That's what determines whether we have a good name or not. "A good name," says one proverb, "is more desirable than great riches; to be esteemed is better than silver and gold" (Proverbs 22:21).

Your name may be in the record books for the most touchdowns at your high school. Your name might be on a bronze plaque on the side of a building testifying that you helped make the construction possible. Your name might be on the door of your business or corporation. You might even become famous enough that people want your autograph. You may be the first woman or first minority person to occupy a prominent position, and your name may be displayed in an honorable place. Your name might also be in places you'd rather forget: arrest records, court cases, divorce certificates.

But ultimately, the most important thing that can ever happen to your name is for God to write it in the Lamb's Book of Life. The Bible is very plain. It says: "if anyone's name is not written there, he will be thrown into the lake of fire" (Revelation 20:15).

So this leads to a very important question: "How can we be sure that our name is written there?" Hear the words of God, and put them into practice:

Not everyone who says to me, 'Lord, Lord,' will en-
ter the kingdom of heaven, but only he who does the
will of my Father who is in heaven. Many will say to

me on that day, 'Lord, Lord, did we not prophesy in
your name, and in your name drive out demons and
perform many miracles?' Then I will tell them plain-
ly, 'I never knew you. Away from me, you evildoers!'
(Matthew 7:21-23)

None of us want to hear the Lord call us an "evildoer." Whoever is checking the Book of Life the day I knock on the gates of
eternity, I'd much rather hear, "Yes, here it is, 'John Michael Helms,'
recorded back in 1972 when you asked the Lord to save you from
your sins. You heard God's words, and you've put them into practice,
and you've been forgiven for the times you didn't. Come in! Come
in! Since you're new here, don't forget to put on your nametag. Jesus
won't need it, but the others here will."

During the Advent season, most of us hope to receive at least
a gift or two with our names on them. As exciting as those moments
are, they last only for a moment. We tear into the package, but in a
few months or years, the gift is usually forgotten. Can you remember what you received for Christmas in 2010? Anything? Come on,
name just one gift. How about 2009? Even if you can, it's not a gift
that'll last forever. One gift that will is eternal life.

The gift comes to us from the one who was spoken of so long
ago by Isaiah who said, "He will be called Wonderful Counselor,
Mighty God, Everlasting Father, Prince of Peace" (Isaiah 9:6).

This Advent, if your name is written in the Lamb's Book of
Life, pause now and thank God for His grace and the gift of eternal
life that has begun in you. If you are not sure whether your name is
written there, then this is a critical hour for you. Peace comes from
knowing that God's promises belong to us. His promise of the Holy
Spirit, our companion of His presence, will be breathed upon us as
soon as we confess Jesus as Lord, meaning He's most important in
our life, repent of our sins, and seek to follow Jesus in a new life of

discipleship. That can happen to you right now.

The promise of heaven is real. The peace of knowing our name is written in the Lamb's Book of Life is real. Advent is a season where we experience His realness now as we look toward December 25. Finding our way is about today and tomorrow. It's not just about what happens to you when you die. Otherwise, this faith journey would be boring, and most of us would get lost along the way.

Advent Actions

1. Go to the website, "First Names and What They Mean." (Find it at www.thefaithlab.com/advent.) Research your first name or those of people you know. How well does your personality reflect the meaning of your name? Do you like what your name means?

2. On the same website, check out the number of celebrities who were born under one name, but later changed their name.

Here's a list of some biblical personalities whose names were changed as a result of meeting God:

Sarai to Sarah ("Argumentative" to "Lady")
Abram to Abraham ("High Father" to "Father of a Multitude")
Jacob to Israel ("Held by the Heel" to "Prince of God")
Simon to Cephas or Peter ("It is Heard" to "Rock")
Saul to Paul ("Borrowed" to "Small")

All these people accepted their name changes because they felt God was calling them to a new life and a new identity. Monks and nuns often take new names when they join a religious order. Popes change their names when they are elected.

The closest thing to a name change many people can relate to is the acceptance of a nickname. Claudia Johnson became known as Lady Bird; Samuel Langhorne Clemens became known as Mark Twain; George Herman Ruth became known as The Babe; and Harriet Tubman became known as Moses.

Do you have a nickname? What does your nickname say about you as a person? If you could change your name, what quality would you want your name to reflect? If God were to change your name, what quality would God want your new name to reflect?

Prayer

God of Eternal Life,

You are the only One who can give the gift of eternal life. We confess that as we move through this world we often become too attached to what's here. We forget that everything earthly is passing away.

We confess to You, Lord, that we fall into the trappings of this world and spend much of our time trying to build a name for ourselves by chasing and accumulating the glitter, glow, and glory of things that will not stand the test of time.

Lord, You have told us what is most important, to love You with all our heart, soul, mind and strength. You have told us to love our neighbor as we love ourselves. These should be our gifts to You, Lord. We know we cannot earn our way to heaven. We trust that by Your grace we have our names written in the Lamb's Book of Life. Even now, may they be written there so that eternal life can begin even now, as we continue to take up our crosses and follow You. Amen.

Caring About the Wrong Things
December 12

I bet some of you are considering buying a new piece of exercise equipment for Christmas. You've looked around the house, and you've already picked out the place where it can go. Here's a news flash: six weeks from the day it arrives, it will be like a museum piece—it'll be looked at, but not touched. You'll get more exercise by walking around it than on it, more muscles by moving it than lifting the weights that come with it. Maybe you'll be the exception.

Many of us have relationships that way. They started out strong, but then we neglect them. We walked around issues we need to address, but found other things to do instead. We've walked around disciplines we knew needed to be a part of our lives, but allowed bad habits to continue instead. Like Jonah, we've walked around responsibilities we knew were ours to carry out, but we left them for others.

Remember Jonah? He's that biblical character God told to go and preach against the great city of Nineveh. Instead, he got on a boat bound for Tarshish. But he never got there. A great storm erupted on the sea. The sailors believed that someone had angered a god, who caused the storm to rage. They threw lots, and the lots pointed to Jonah. With great irony, the author shows that the superstition of the sailors was true; someone had angered a god.

Jonah admitted he had angered the God—the God of heaven who made the sea and land. He told the sailors to throw him overboard, and the sea would become calm. Amazingly, Jonah would rather die than change his ways.

I've seen people like that, haven't you? The physician has said, "If you don't change your lifestyle, you are going to die." The financial advisor has said, "If you don't change your spending habits, you are going bankrupt." The educator has said, "If you don't study hard and earn a degree, chances are you will be poor." The judge has said, "If you don't obey the law, you are going to die, and take others with you." The preacher has said, "If you don't love the Lord your God with all your heart, soul, mind, and strength, and love your neighbor as yourself, you are going to lose your soul." And yet, no change is made. People continue to travel the wide road of destruction. Have you ever known Jonah? Are you Jonah?

Exercise equipment in the living room will not change your body unless it's used as recommended. Good advice from doctors, financial advisors, and educators is of little value unless we apply it all. And the knowledge of God's love will be as useless as Confederate money if we don't embody it and share it, even with those people we don't like.

After Jonah chose death instead of sharing God's message with the Ninevites, God sent His personal escort service, a great fish, to transport Jonah to the shores of Nineveh, where he was unceremoniously vomited to the beach. With great reluctance, he went into the city. In Hebrew, his message is a grand total of five words. In English, the translation is only a few more: "Forty more days and Nineveh will be overturned."

That's it. A five-word sermon. Some of you have waited all your life to hear a five-word sermon. But what good can five words do?

Look what happened: The Ninevites believed God. They declared a fast for all of them, from the least to the greatest. When God saw how they turned from their evil ways, He had compassion and did not bring upon them the destruction He had threatened.

God had compassion on the people of Nineveh. But Jonah never did. At the end of this short story, Jonah is a pathetic figure. He's angered by the transformation he sees happening in the city because he hated the Ninevites. He didn't want them to receive mercy, only destruction. The news makes him sick—so sick he's ready to die—again. He goes outside the city, makes himself a shelter, and sits down.

God allows a vine to grow up into a shelter that provides Jonah shade from the hot sun. But the next day God sends a worm that eats the vine and it withers. When the scorching sun comes out, Jonah is miserable and angry. God asks him if he has a right to be angry about the withered vine and Jonah says: "I do. I am angry enough to die" (Jonah 4:9).

> *Then the Lord said, 'You have been concerned about this vine, though you did not tend it or make it grow. It sprang up overnight and died overnight. But Nineveh has more than a hundred and twenty thousand people who cannot tell their right hand from their left, and many cattle as well. Should I not be concerned about this great city?'(Jonah 4:10-11).*

To teach his audiences how easy it is to become more concerned about the least important issue, Tony Campolo, a Baptist evangelist and college professor, has been known to begin many of his speeches by telling his audience that while they were sleeping the evening before, more than 30,000 kids had died of starvation related to malnutrition. Then he'd tell his audience that they "didn't give a damn." Then he'd tell his audience that they were more upset because he just used an expletive than they were about the fact that 30,000 kids had died the night before from malnutrition.

What upsets you? What consumes you? What needs of

others ignite your passions to do something to make a difference in their lives? What needs of humanity drive you to get up off the couch and exercise your spiritual gifts so you will make a difference in their lives? What prejudices do you still hold that cause you to steer clear of ministry the Lord has directed you to carry out? Whom do you despise to the point that you would go in the other direction rather than share with them the kindness and grace of the Lord?

If you are afraid to answer these questions honestly, it's a sign you are running, just like Jonah, away from the Lord. If you answer them, but refuse to go where the Lord has instructed you, and do what the Lord has instructed you to do, it's a sign that you care, like Jonah, about the wrong things.

The season of Advent provides many opportunities to focus on the needs of others, both spiritual and physical. Yet if we aren't careful, we can get more upset that we've run out of wrapping paper than the fact that our neighbors on the other side of town have run out of diapers and milk. If we aren't careful, our prejudices will dictate whom we invite to church and whom we see as people worthy of the Kingdom of God. Instead, we should acknowledge our prejudices and repent of them, understanding that God's kingdom and His grace are deep and wide. Jonah never acknowledged this. Instead, he decided he would rather drown in the deep and wide ocean.

God showed his unique fishing technique after the great fish spit Jonah out on the beach of Nineveh. I suppose God could fish us out of any number of the deep crevices where we attempt to hide from His call. But there's really no need. He's plunged Himself into our lives in the most vulnerable, real, and visible way possible, when the baby Jesus was born in Bethlehem.

During His adult ministry, He plunged himself into the lives of humanity to demonstrate the heart of God. Not only did He choose disciples then, but He's still looking for disciples now.

Should we decide like Jonah to go the other way, He's not

likely to drag us ashore with an ultimatum. Rather, as with the rich young ruler who refused to sell his possessions and give them to the poor and follow Jesus, He'll just let us go our own way.

As we continue to move through Advent, God will present us with opportunities of ministry as His disciples. With each one we must decide whether we will go the other way or help show others the way of our Lord. Our decisions will clearly indicate what it is and whom it is that we care about the most.

Advent Actions

1. Pick up a button, a rock, a thimble—something small and odd that you would not normally carry—and place it in your pocket or purse this day as a reminder that we often care about the wrong things. When you come across this object, ask yourself, "Am I caring about the right things today? Am I treating others as being more important than myself this Advent? Is there anywhere God has asked me to go that I am not going? Is there anything God has asked me to do that I am not doing?"

2. Find one worthwhile ministry this Advent to be involved in that is out of your comfort zone. Feed the hungry at a soup kitchen. Visit the elderly at a nursing home. Work at a food bank. Wrap presents for free. Deliver food to shut-ins. Volunteer at an animal shelter.

Prayer

God of Change,

Change happens all around us all the time. The seasons change. We age.

Nothing remains the same Lord, except You. You are always coming to us in fresh ways. We don't usually like change unless it happens slowly. When You ask us to do something new, something out of our comfort zone, we have a tendency to become like Jonah; we disobey. God of change, You sent the Christ Child for everyone, not just us. We confess that we wrap Him up in swaddling clothes and pass Him around among friends to the exclusion of those people who are not like us. Lord, we are Jonah. Tell us. Where is Nineveh? Where do You want us to go with your message of love and grace? Amen.

Immanuel:
The Most Important Word in the Bible
December 13

During the darkest hours of World War II in England, a gloom swept over the nation as the Luftwaffe dropped tons and tons of bombs on London. There was a legitimate fear felt for the safety of King George VI and his family. His staff, therefore, made secret arrangements to transport the king and his family to safety in Canada for the duration of the war. Despite the urging of his advisors, George refused to leave his country in its darkest hour.

Shortly thereafter, an incident was reported in a London newspaper in which the king was inspecting a bombed out section of London after an air raid. While walking through the rubble, an elderly man walked up to King George and said, "You, here in the midst of this? You are indeed a good King!"

That's how we should view Jesus. As the Magi came to worship Him, we must remember that Jesus was God incarnate. God chose to come to us in such a personal way. "God! You're in the middle of this? In a cattle stall? Born to a poor young Jewish girl? You are indeed a good King!"[11]

The Bible clearly shows us a God who has been involved in our salvation history and has demonstrated to us, in His most personal and dramatic way through Jesus that He wanted to be WITH US through the joys and the struggles of life.

Walk with me briefly through the pages of biblical history, which demonstrates the truth of the name Immanuel, "God with us!"

To Abraham God said, "Do not be afraid, for I am with you; I will bless you and will increase the number of your descendants for the sake of my servant Abraham" (Genesis 23:24).

To Moses, God said, "I will be with you. And this will be the sign to you that it is I who have sent you: When you have brought the people out of Egypt, you will worship God on this mountain" (Exodus 3:12).

To the Hebrews, Moses said: "Do not be afraid. God has come to test you, so that the fear of God will be with you to keep you from sinning" (Exodus 20:20).

To Joshua, God said: "As I was with Moses, so I will be with you; I will never leave you nor forsake you" (Joshua 1:5).

When the angel of the LORD appeared to Gideon, he said: "The LORD is with you, mighty warrior" (Judges 6:12).

To Saul, God said: "The Spirit of the LORD will come upon you in power, and you will prophesy with them; and you will be changed into a different person. Once these signs are fulfilled, do whatever your hand finds to do, for God is with you" (1 Samuel 10:6-7).

To Jeremiah, God said: "Do not say, 'I am only a child.' You must go to everyone I send you to and say whatever I command you. Do not be afraid of them, for I am with you and will rescue you,' declares the LORD" (Jeremiah 1:7-8).

To Amos, God said: "Seek good, not evil, that you may live. Then the LORD God Almighty will be with you, just as you say he is" (Amos 5:14).

From the book of Haggai: "Then Haggai, the LORD's messenger, gave this message of the LORD to the people: 'I am with you,' declares the LORD" (Haggai 1:13-14).

Throughout Old Testament history, God's presence was felt and made known among the Hebrew people. So it should not be surprising that in "the fullness of time" when God chose to come and be present in the flesh, the angel said that the baby's name should be "Immanuel," which means, "God with us."

Like King George, who walked through the rubble of a bombed out section of London; Jesus, Immanuel, God incarnate, came to walk through the rubble of humanity for our sakes.

His own life was not His concern, but rather the redemption of our souls. When He was put to death on the cross, even the Roman centurion overseeing the affair said, "Surely, this was a righteous man" (Luke 23:47).

Jesus' death could have been the end. Death could have ended it all. Because Jesus arose from the dead, He can be with us today through His Holy Spirit. This is the reason "Immanuel" (God with us) is the most important word in the Bible. The resurrection proved that the birth in Bethlehem was indeed the birth of Immanuel.

When Jesus ascended into heaven, He breathed upon His disciples the gift of the Holy Spirit. The Holy Spirit is Immanuel. Through God's gift of the Holy Spirit, God is with those who profess Jesus as Lord and Savior of their lives.

Through the challenge of the Great Commission, Jesus gave His disciples authority in heaven and on earth to:

> *Go and make disciples of all nations, baptizing them in the name of the Father and of the Son and of the Holy Spirit, and teaching them to obey everything I have commanded you. And surely I am with you always, to the very end of the age (Matthew 28:19-20).*

As you find your way through Advent, one of the most awesome concepts to remember is that the God who journeyed with Haggai, Amos, Jeremiah, Samuel, Gideon, Joshua, Moses, the Hebrews, and Abraham will also journey with you.

The gift of the Holy Spirit makes this possible. You will not find this gift under a tree, but our Lord hung on a tree so that we might have this gift. God raised Jesus to new life to make it all possible. Now believe. Accept this gift by faith, for this is how you find your way to life abundant and life eternal. This is the path to peace.

Advent Actions

1. Interview three children of any age. Tell them you have some homework to do and that as your assignment you have to interview a child and ask a few questions about God. Here are the questions:

Do you believe that God is with people all the time? Is God with you? If the child answers "yes," ask: How do you know that God is with you? Can you give me an example?

Did you know that God said that Jesus would also be called Immanuel, which means "God with us"? If the child answers, "no," ask: Do you believe God is with you? How do you know?

2. I'm curious what you learned. Send me a postcard with your answers: Dr. Michael Helms, FBC Jefferson, 81 Institute Street, Jefferson, GA 30549.

3. During the Christmas holidays you might have the opportunity to say a prayer before a family meal. It's a good opportunity to give a quick testimony of thanksgiving for God being with you through the year. You might summarize how God was with various people through biblical history up to the birth of Christ. Then you might describe how God has been with and your family and finish with a prayer. If you get long winded with food waiting, no one will hear you. Keep it brief.

Prayer

Immanuel,

Were it not for Your Holy Spirit, how would we know You were with us? We would be like those of the Old Testament, afraid that Your presence might be among us for a while, only to feel an emptiness later. Thank You for the gift of your Holy Spirit, our deposit, the guarantee of our relationship with You. We claim the promise of Jesus who said that He would never leave us or forsake us.

While we feel removed and distant from You at times, Immanuel, we know that is because our sin separates us from You. We know that You are with us, seeking to restore us to a right relationship with You.

We praise You that You are with us, when we win and when we lose, when we walk upright and when we fall, when we find joy and when we grieve, when we put others first and when we think only of ourselves, when we complain and when we are thankful, when we dream and when we accept things as they are. You are with us always, even to the end of the age.

Our problem, Immanuel, is that we are not always with You. You've invited us to follow You. But there are some places we haven't made up our minds to go with You yet. Immanuel, don't stop asking. As long as You stay with us, there's still hope that we will eventually go with You where You want us to go. Amen.

Don't Let the Stress of the Season Steal Your Joy
December 14

So you just got home from a day of Christmas shopping. If you had any Christmas cheer, it's all but gone now. Every light that could have turned red did. Two people turned in front of you as if they owned the road, almost causing a collision. You drove around the parking lot at the mall for ten minutes looking for a parking place. You ended up parking a country mile from the nearest entrance. The only gift that was left like the one you wanted was a display model, and the manager would not sell it to you.

After deciding on an alternative gift, you waited in line for thirty minutes, only to discover that the UPC code was scanned in at a price twenty dollars higher than was displayed. To get the price corrected, you had to wait while the manager was called again, holding up the frustrated line of people behind you. Once you got home, you discovered that the small print on the box that read, "Some assembly required," was an understatement. It should have read, "Must have an engineering degree from Georgia Tech in order to assemble." Once assembled, of course, you discovered that you purchased the wrong size batteries, meaning you'd have to make another trip into the shopping jungle.

This hasn't happened to me in a long time. Except for my local shopping, I now do a lot of my shopping from the quiet, peaceful abode of my living room. I compare prices on the Internet, make a few selections with the click of my mouse, and say goodbye to all that stress. I try to do most of this before Thanksgiving or catch the Thanksgiving specials.

During Advent, as we prepare for the coming of Christmas Day, stress has a tendency to spike. Most of us have all the normal responsibilities of life to tend to. In addition to our normal schedules, we try to fit in more work so we can have some time off. We have parties to attend, gifts to buy, homes to decorate, food to prepare, bags to pack if we are traveling, houses to clean if people are coming over, and relationships to maintain.

Do you have your share of stress this Advent? If so, take heart. The first Christmas wasn't stress free either. The scripture says that when the angel Gabriel appeared to Mary she was "greatly troubled at his words" (Luke 1:29). She was not overjoyed, not floating on a cloud, not excited, but troubled—"greatly troubled." Even after the angel told her what was to take place, her anxieties did not subside: "How will this be since I am still a virgin?" (Luke 1:34) she asked.

Though Mary believed the angel, she obviously wondered how the news would be shared, and how others would react. How did it come about that she was the one chosen to carry this child? How would Joseph respond?

Speaking of Joseph, he had his own problems. He had to make a decision about what to do with Mary. Talk about stress! Here's a man who obviously loves his bride-to-be, but finds out she's pregnant. What a gut-wrenching decision he had to face. He had a choice of three acts: He could have had her publicly disgraced and the law fully applied to her—death by stoning. He could have quietly divorced her. Engagement carried the kind of legal commitment we equate with marriage. He could still have married her, a choice that apparently never received any serious consideration until the Lord got involved. It seems that Joseph was going to quietly divorce her.

Through an angel, God revealed His plans to Joseph. God calmed Joseph's fears. God didn't take away all Joseph's stress, but

He let Joseph know that whatever the situation, God could be depended on to see him through. God's presence gave Joseph the confidence and wisdom to make the right decision.

If it were not for the Lord intervening and interrupting our stress-filled lives with words of comfort and encouragement, and providing us with a sense of peace and presence in the midst of this chaotic and broken world, we would make wrong choices detrimental to our future and to the future of others. December 25 would come and go, and we would be so caught up in the brokenness of our world that we'd never really celebrate the birth of Jesus or its significance for our lives. Are you in danger of this happening to you?

As Mary and Joseph made their way to the town of Bethlehem as required by the decree of Caesar Augustus, it's very likely they were hurting, lonely, and scared. There were so many unknown factors and unanswered questions: "Why couldn't God have chosen a more convenient time for this child to be born? Will we find any friends or old family members in Bethlehem to help us? What if the baby comes while we are traveling? Who will help us deliver this child? Where will we stay?"

Don't you see? When we see manger scenes, we see joy. But joy came in the midst of uncertainty, struggle, stress, and unanswered questions. Joy still comes that way.

The world wants to gobble up our joy. The world wants to swallow our joy into its deep abyss. But God has had a plan from the beginning of time to give us joy. From the very beginning of time when the earth was formless and empty, when darkness was over the surface of the deep, the Spirit of God was present, hovering over the waters (Genesis 1:2). This same Spirit hovers over our darkness. Whenever we reach out to touch the hand of God, light makes its way into our lives. Joy happens.

Joy is possible, not because there is no struggle; joy is possible because Jesus is in the midst of our struggle, pushing the darkness aside, stirring the Living Waters of life, bringing peace and comfort to our souls.

Like Mary, we may start out greatly troubled, but because of God's Spirit, we can pull back and put life in perspective, pondering things in our hearts. That's when we realize that even in the midst of stressful times, times of uncertainty, and struggle, unlike many others, those of us who know Christ can have "joy, joy, joy, joy, down in our hearts, down in our hearts to stay" (George W. Cooke).

Advent Actions

1. Complete the <u>Life Event Score for Stress Indicator</u>.

Death of Spouse 100
Divorce 73
Marital Separation 65
Death of Close
    Family Member 63
Jail Term 63
Personal Injury/Illness 53
Alcoholism/Drug
    Addiction in Family 50
Fired 47
Retired 45
Reconciliation 45
Ill Health of
    Family Member 44
Pregnancy 40
Childbirth 39
Sex Difficulties 39
Financial Change 38
Different Job 36
Increased Arguments
    with Spouse 35
Debt or Mortgage 31
Motor Accident 30
In-Law Trouble 29
Child Leaving Home 29
Outstanding Achievement ... 28

Child Starting/
    Leaving School 26
Spouse Starting/
    Stopping Work 26
Change in Alcohol
    Consumption 25
Change in Religion 25
Change in Smoking
    Habits 24
Change in Work
    Hours 23
Change with Boss 23
Change in Sport/
    Exercise 20
Change in Recreation 20
Change in Residence 20
Change in Social Activity 18
Change in Amount
    of Sleep 16
Change in Eating/
    Weight 15
Prolonged Travel/
    Vacation 13
Minor law Violation 10
Score _____ If above 200,
your stress is above average.[12]

2. Read Appendix 2, "Living a Balanced Life."

3. Remember stress is a part of life. No life is without stress. The engine of a car is designed to handle stress, but if over-stressed it will overheat and break down.

It's important to maintain a balanced life. When life gets out of balance, we need to know when to allow qualified people to help us with our load and find our way back to good decision-making.

Prayer

God of Balance,

I've read that if You had placed the earth one degree closer or farther away from the sun, life could not exist here. You knew just the right balance for life. We live sometimes not knowing the right balance for our lives. We move through our day without consulting You. We ignore Your instructions in the Bible. A lot of our stress is brought on by disobedience.

There are others of us, Lord, who try to do everything we can to follow Your instructions. In fact, some of our stress is the stress of ministry. We are like the Psalmist who observed that those who did not fear God seemed to have:

> ...no struggles; their bodies are healthy and strong.
> They are free from the burdens common to man; they
> are not plagued by human ills...Surely in vain have I
> kept my heart pure; in vain have I washed my hands
> in innocence. All day long I have been plagued; I have
> been punished every morning (Psalm 73:4-5; 13-14).

Like the Psalmist, Lord, we need a fresh perspective. We need Your help in bringing the stresses of life back into proper balance. Send that help in the form of a trusted friend, time alone, rest, quality time with family, worship, exercise, a healthy diet, healing from addictive behaviors, or counsel from a pastor or a counseling professional. If we just need to reevaluate our priorities and return to spiritual disciplines, help us change our ways and bring balance back to our lives. Amen.

Finding Hope within a Dark World
December 15

During the early 1960s, our country began riding a wave of optimism and hope that was driven mainly by a young, charismatic president named John F. Kennedy. This man was helping the country navigate some of the our nation's most serious problems: the Cuban missile crisis, the rise of Communism, the challenges of Russia as a world superpower, civil unrest between blacks and whites, and the growing conflict in Vietnam. In spite of such a long list of problems, our country had confidence in their young leader.

If you are old enough to remember when President Kennedy was assassinated, you probably recall where you were when you heard the news. That day, hopes were dashed. Our country grieved. Two days later, Jack Ruby shot Kennedy's assassin, Lee Harvey Oswald. Conspiracy theories have been with us ever since.

With the release of the motion picture "Bobby," our minds have once again been thrust back to the decade of the sixties. We are reminded that if it were not for another assassin's bullet, another Kennedy may have made it to 1600 Pennsylvania Avenue North West. Bobby Kennedy, JFK's brother, served as Attorney General under his brother before being elected senator from New York. He was killed only moments after delivering a speech celebrating his victory in the 1968 California Democratic Presidential primary.

Only three months prior to Bobby Kennedy's death, Martin Luther King, Jr., was assassinated while standing on the balcony of his motel room in Memphis, Tennessee, where he was to lead a pro-test march in sympathy with striking garbage workers of that city. Meanwhile, soldiers continued to die in Vietnam.

It didn't matter if you were black or white, young or old, rich or poor, in the 1960s, you were looking for assurances that the world wasn't going to fall apart. People were looking for signs of tranquility and peace. The hippie movement began, and youth culture turned to drugs and sex, seeking an escape from the pain of the world because it seemed that there was nothing but pain, war, and death all around them.

When I was a teenager in the 1970s, our nation was at the peak of the Cold War. Relations with Russia were strained to the point that I wondered if a nuclear war would one day occur. We watched films at school that taught us how to respond in the event of such an attack. I had a real fear that a nuclear war would happen in my lifetime and that life as we knew it would one day end with a nuclear attack.

Since then, signs of hope have emerged in our world, but not without setbacks. The world continues to be a volatile place, and its future is still uncertain. North Korea recently tested a nuclear bomb. Iran is getting closer to developing a bomb, a country that's openly hostile to Israel and to the United States. Today, more than fearing a direct attack from a bomb on a missile, experts tell us that we are more at risk from a dirty bomb, a nuclear bomb smuggled into our country by terrorists or one actually made in this country by terror-ists.

All this apocalyptic talk depresses me, and I'd rather avoid it. Some ministers thrive on it and often preach from texts that speak about end times. Some will even read passages of scripture and infer from those texts that we are in the last days, saying the world as we know it will end soon, in our lifetime even.

I'm not that smart. Frankly, I'm not one who's asking God

to end His world soon. Despite all the suffering in this world, I am grateful for life, and I'm in no hurry for it to end. I suppose if I were one of the ones suffering greatly, I'd be thinking more about paradise. Even so, apocalyptic scripture, scripture that deals with end times, is a part of the Bible. We must recognize that the world we know will one day pass away.

As we focus on Advent, it's appropriate to think about the advent of the end. Mark 13 teaches that one day the world as we know it will fall apart, completely. Even if it doesn't happen in our lifetime, our individual worlds will end. It happens every day to somebody, somewhere. It will happen today. It will happen tomorrow. As sure as the sun rises in the east and sets in the west, somebody's world is ending right now.

At the time Jesus was born there had been better times in Judah. The days of King David and Solomon were, of course, Israel's greatest days. No country ruled over them. The Jewish world crumbled when the Assyrians took control of Israel. It crumbled again when the Babylonians took control of Judah, occupied Jerusalem, and destroyed the temple, carrying thousands of people away into exile. Later it was the Romans who conquered their region. They were still there when Jesus was born.

King Herod, who was half Jewish, in an attempt to appease the Jews, had the temple rebuilt. When the temple was completed, it was the largest site of its kind in the ancient world. Its wall stood 80 feet. Its area encompassed 172,000 square yards. The historian Josephus tells us there was so much gold on the temple that when the sun shined on it, it was blinding to look at.

Jesus' own disciples were sucked into the awe of that man-made structure. "One day as they were leaving the temple they marveled at the structure and said to Jesus, 'Look, Teacher! What massive stones! What magnificent buildings!'" (Mark 1:13).

How quickly the disciples had forgotten that the last

temple had been destroyed! The implication here is that the disciples were looking at the structure as a permanent fortress, something that could last forever. The temple was their security that their world could never fall apart again.

So Jesus laid the bad news on them: "Do you see these great buildings? Not one stone here will be left on another; every one will be thrown down" (Mark 13:2). Jesus was telling the disciples that their world was going to fall apart, again.

Later as they sat on the Mount of Olives and looked down on the temple, Jesus went on to explain to Peter, James, John, and Andrew what could be expected in those turbulent days: deceivers, that is, those claiming to be saviors; war; earthquakes; famines; suffering from floggings; the gospel preached to the nations; hate among family members; and the destruction of Jewish society.

Jesus sat with the first four men He called to ministry, giving them mostly depressing news. It was not what they signed on as disciples to hear. They signed on to hear about things getting better, not about things getting worse. The news was depressing, as depressing as hearing that a President had been shot. Their hopes were dashed. Their dreams were shattered, but at least they still had Jesus for a while longer.

What about the people who first read Mark's gospel? These people were reading this after the destruction of the temple. Their world had already fallen apart. By AD 70, the words of Jesus had come true. One of the worst and bloodiest wars for the Jewish people occurred in that year as the Romans came and demolished the city of Jerusalem and killed the people. Many Christians fled to the hills to escape.

By this time, disciples of Jesus had suffered beatings and other hardships just as Jesus predicted. False prophets had been among them gathering followers. It had been as Jesus said. The people who read Mark's gospel, therefore, read the words of a credible Lord.

Their world had fallen apart as Jesus had said it would.

Since that day, the world has continued to fall apart: drugs, AIDS, a gunshot in the night, splintered families, wars, loss of pension plans, hunger, corruption in government, and sexual immorality have all caused people's worlds to fall apart.

Many people look at our nation the way the disciples looked at the stones of the temple: massive, immovable, indestructible. Don't be fooled. It can fall. The cracks are showing from within. Some of you may be optimistic and say that our country, our world even, is a better place to live than it was thirty years ago. You can point to the fall of communism in all but a few nations, the end of the Cold War, and the fall of the Berlin Wall. There have also been just as many setbacks: the bombing of the Federal Building in Oklahoma City, September 11, the Wars in Iraq and Afghanistan, the failure to take care of Hurricane Katrina victims, a growing threat of a holy war waged by Islamic Fundamentalists, and renewed fighting between Israel and Hamas, just to name a few.

Isn't the season of Advent supposed to be one of hope and expectation? I haven't painted a very hopeful picture so far, have I?

I want you to be a hopeful individual today, but I want you to put your hope in the right place. I can jump off a building into a Dixie cup and hope it's going to support my weight, but that hope is going to get me killed. We have too many people placing their hope in the things of this world. If our hope is in a temple or a President, in the stock market or in our government, these things are not going to hold up. These worlds are going to crumble. Sooner or later, they will all come to an end.

Can you sing these words with author Edward Mote?
My hope is built on
nothing less
Than Jesus' blood and righteousness.

I dare not trust the
sweetest frame
But wholly trust in Jesus' Name

Can you affirm these words of the Psalmist?

Find rest, O my soul, in God alone; my hope comes
from him. He alone is my rock and my salvation; he is
my fortress, I will not be shaken. My salvation and my
honor depend on God; he is my mighty rock, my ref-
uge. Trust in him at all times, O people; pour out your
hearts to him, for God is our refuge (Psalm 62:5-8).

As we get closer to the date that we celebrate the birth of the Christ Child, Jesus remains our hope. The same One who was the hope of the world for the disciples, the same Christ who was the hope of the early church after the temple was destroyed, the same Christ who was our hope the day Pearl Harbor was attacked, the same Christ who was our hope the day President Kennedy was shot, the same Christ who was our hope on September 11, 2001—that same Christ is our hope today.

If our world lay in ruins, I can assure you that news of Christ's return would sound better to you than it might today. For the people who first read the gospel of Mark, their world was in ruins, and there was renewed hope to hear of the promise that Jesus would return.

His return, of course, is a matter of God's timing, not ours. Jesus said as soon as the twigs of the fig tree get tender and its leaves come out, you know that summer is near. Summer is a season of optimism. So the season in which Jesus returns will be an uplifting time for Christians. In spite of all the tragedy that will be going on in the world, Christians have the assurance that God has a plan to redeem those who are in Christ Jesus. This is another reason we do not have to dread the advent of end times. We can be optimistic and not despairing.

The scriptures tell us to watch and to work. It seems that each generation thinks Jesus is coming back in its lifetime. During colonial times in New England, state legislators panicked as an unexpected solar eclipse occurred. Some thought it marked the end of the world.

A motion was made to adjourn. However, one wise man said, "Mr. Speaker, if it is not the end of the world and we adjourn, we shall appear to be fools. If it is the end of the world, I should choose to be found doing my duty. I move you, sir, that candles be brought."[13]

This is the idea: Jesus commands us to work, to do our duty, to carry out our task, working for a better world. In doing so, we are more likely to work for things that matter most, things that make a difference in this world and in the world to come. Therefore, I move that candles be brought in so we can continue our work. Let us do our work with the hope of His advent, His second coming. Amen.

Advent Actions

1. Tonight, light a candle, and think about the work you are doing in the name of Christ. Get the family involved. Ask family members to light a candle and name one area of work/life they are involved in, and ask God to bless that in the upcoming year.

2. Pick up the daily paper, and do a quick review. Notice all the bad news in the paper, and think about the loss of hope this news brings to those people who are directly affected. Remember that the return of Jesus will also be a loss of hope to all those who do not know Him as Lord. Ask God to help you remember that there is an urgency to share the love of God with those who do not know Him.

Prayer

God of the Second Advent,

Peter writes that You have delayed Your return because You are patient and You desire as many people as possible to know You. You have instructed us to "keep watch" because we do not know the day or the hour of Your return (Matt. 25:13). We do not believe that You meant for us to sit around and literally watch, Lord. Rather, our watching shall be an active watch. As we work, play, and go about our lives, we shall keep it on our minds that "today Jesus may come."

Lord, if we live expectantly, it will not change Your timetable, but it will change how we live. That is, after all, what You want to happen, isn't it? You want the Second Advent to change us, even before it occurs. May it be so, Lord. May it be so. Amen.

An Unexpected Visitor on Moving Day
December 16

Jesus showed up the day I was moving across town from one house to another. It was a surprise visit. Jesus has a way of showing up when you least expect Him. Sometimes I feel like saying, "Why don't You at least call before You drop by? That way I can"— he interrupted me and finished my sentence—"hide things you don't want me to see or start doing something spiritual?"

"I wasn't going to say that," I said. "I know," He responded, "but that's what you were thinking." What was I supposed to say to that?

A friend commented to me recently that moving is really a personal thing. I think I know what she meant. It's the packing that's personal. We will gladly accept help with the moving. As long as we are moving things that people usually see anyway, it's no big deal. But it's a little different to go through drawers, closets, the attic, and the garage with a friend standing around, who can witness everything you've saved over the last ten years. It can be embarrassing.

So, when Jesus showed up as I was going through a decade's worth of stuff, I wasn't comfortable. "You know there are times during my day that I'm so busy I hardly even stop to think about You being around," I confessed to Jesus. "Why is it that I'm so aware of Your presence on moving day?"

"I like moving day," Jesus said. "Remember, I was born on the move," he said with a bit of nostalgia in His voice. I hadn't thought much about that, but Jesus was, you know, born on the move. Mary, nine months pregnant, had to leave her home in Nazareth along with Joseph, the man she married, and together they traveled to Bethlehem, the city of Joseph's birth, because Caesar Augustus had ordered each man to return to the place of his birth to be taxed.

Not long after the birth of Jesus, the family of three was on the move again, this time to Egypt, to escape the hatred of King Herod. The king had heard of the birth of Jesus through astrologers from the East who had come to worship Jesus and bring Him gifts. After the astrologers did not return to tell the king where baby Jesus could be found, King Herod ordered that males under the age of two in the area be put to death. Warned by an angel in a dream, Joseph moved the family to Egypt.

A couple of years later the family was on the move again. This time, they returned to Nazareth, where Jesus was raised and lived until his ministry years. When He began His years of ministry, Jesus stayed on the move, apparently giving up a permanent home, once commenting that the Son of Man had "no place to lay his head" (Matthew 8:20).

So Jesus, I suppose, had some affinity for moving day, even though not all His moves were pleasant. So, why was I not very thrilled that He'd shown up at my house as I packed my belongings?

It wasn't that His company was all bad. There were times that day that I found pleasure in Jesus' company, especially as we went through many items that belonged to my children. As I rummaged through my sons' trophies, medals and photographs, we talked about YMCA soccer, diving meets, and R.A. derby races. "The years fly by so quickly, Jesus. My boys have grown up in this house. Thank You for the fun times we've had here." I might have even shed a tear or two as I packed away all those memories.

Then I started packing some of my stuff. In one box I packed twenty-five hats. "Twenty-five hats? Why do you need twenty-five hats?" Jesus asked. "You have only one head." I made no attempt to explain my fetish for hats. In another box I packed over fifty ties. "Wow!" Jesus exclaimed. "What does that come to? That's over $1000 worth of ties." "No way," I said. "Well, you've got over fifty, and it's almost impossible to purchase a tie for under $20. You do the math."

The universe was designed through Him, so I figured there wasn't any need in figuring. I'd just never thought about how much money I'd spent on ties. I started thinking about how many of them I never wear, and yet ties catch my eyes at clothing stores every time I go.

Jesus pointed to one of my wiser purchases, the fireproof safe. Years ago I housed my guns away from the children and thieves, and placed all my important papers and other small valuables in the safe in case of fire. I decided I would wait until Jesus left to deal with the contents of the safe—too personal. It didn't matter. He brought up the safe and the contents anyway.

"Nice safe," he said. "That was one of your better purchases. It's always good to keep weapons out of reach of children and thieves. By the way, how many guns do you have in there now, anyway?" As I began to name the caliber rifles and the different gauge shotguns, it began to dawn on me that I wasn't doing this for His benefit. I was catching on. Jesus always uses questions the way a surgeon uses a scalpel.

"What kind of gun was that you bought last year?" he asked. I explained that it was a Mossberg 12-gauge pump, full choke that shoots 2 3/4" or 3" shells. I bought it because I really didn't have a true turkey shotgun. "How many turkeys have you killed with your 16-gauge Mossberg pump?" he asked. "About six." I said. "Sounds like a true turkey shotgun to me," Jesus said.

"I guess you hunted a lot with your new gun last year?" Jesus inquired. "Well, actually no. But I hope to next season. You see I had all these bonus points on my Bass Pro Shop credit card so I could purchase anything in the store with those points"—once again Jesus interrupted—"so you bought something you otherwise wouldn't have been able to buy?" "Exactly!" I countered. Now I knew He understood.

"Did it ever occur to you to purchase something for someone else? Wasn't there anything you could have purchased to help get someone through a difficult time or something you could have bought and given away just as a way of saying, 'Thanks' or 'I love you' or 'Keep up the good work'? You know, since it wasn't costing you anything."

Jesus can be really irritating sometimes. His probing questions were beginning to bother me. "Jesus," I said, "If You had to show up on a day like this, couldn't You just have come over to help me move?" Jesus replied, "My son, that's exactly why I came."

It was then I remembered a passage of scripture I learned years ago, "For where your treasure is, there will your heart be also" (Matthew 6:21, NIV). In other words, our hearts follow our wallets. I don't want my heart following, what can be boxed up, loaded on a truck, and rolled down the highway. I want my heart to follow what can be stored in heaven, what can change a life for eternity, what can relieve human suffering on earth now, what can bring a smile to the face of a child, what can provide comfort and company to the aging, what can bring a lifetime of change to a wayward soul, even change for eternity. I really do want that, but I've got some moving to do.

Advent Actions

Sit down as a family and talk about this topic: "Stuff." As a family discuss the following:

1. If the contents of your home were to catch fire and you had time to carry only three things out of the house, what three things would you carry out and why?

After all have had time to name the items they would carry out of the house, analyze what each person chose. Did anyone choose items based on their dollar value alone? Did anyone choose items because they had sentimental value? Did anyone have problems deciding? If so, why? Do you have a lot of things that mean nothing to you that you could easily live without? How much of our money do we spend on those things that we could easily live without?

2. Do you have a garage? Is it so full of stuff that you can't park your automobile in it? If that's not you, I'm sure you know someone like that. Why do we collect so much stuff? What stuff do you collect? When is the collecting of stuff a good thing, and when does it become a bad thing?

3. What's the difference between you having stuff and stuff having you?

4. If Jesus were to make an unexpected visit to your home, what stuff would you be ashamed for Him to see at Your house? What would you hide? What would you be proud to show Him? What doors would you close?

5. Now it's the time of the year we usually go out and purchase more stuff. Don't wait until moving day to rethink how much stuff you collect.

Prayer

God of Majesty and Simplicity,

Forgive us all for focusing on the material aspects of the season. We are reminded that the Son of Man had nowhere to lay His head. Having a roof over ours never seems to be enough. Most of us have more stuff than we will ever need or use. We need to live simpler lives. Simpler lives will bring more peace and less stress. May there not be a single material thing that has a grip on us, Lord. Help us to be more giving and less self-centered. This Advent, help us to remember that only that which we give away will be credited to our account in heaven. Amen.

Passing Over the Most Valuable Item
December 17

The picture of Jesus with a child on His lap and children at His feet was placed in the middle of $120 worth of merchandise from Wal-Mart. The "store" was set up and ready for the children on the last day of revival services. They brought play money with them to purchase the items. Through the week they had earned play money for answering questions about Bible stories told by the evangelist.

Sometimes he would give them a dollar of play money for answering an easy question or just for trying. The difficulty of the question determined the amount of play money he gave them. Harder answers might push the reward up to ten dollars! The big payoff went to the child who could explain the main point of the biblical story. The children came every night, excited and motivated. They listened attentively. Each night they lined their pockets with more play money. More money meant more stuff could be purchased on the last night. Like kids waiting for Christmas morning, they waited impatiently on the last night of the revival for the store to open to purchase the candy and toys.

Finally, the doors were opened. The small candy bars cost a dollar in play money. The Match Box cars sold for five dollars. The dolls sold for fifteen dollars. The ball and bat sold for twenty dollars. One by one, the children made their choices and used their play money to purchase the items that sported highly inflated prices to match the amount of money earned by the children.

The picture of Jesus with the children was in the middle of the table. The evangelist was going to give it to the first child who inquired about its cost. He was going to say, "I'm glad you asked about that picture. What do you think Jesus costs?" Perhaps the child would respond with a guess to which the evangelist would have said, "Child, Jesus doesn't cost you anything. All you have to do is ask for Him." But no one asked about Jesus. Amid all the candy and toys, Jesus took a back seat. He was ignored.

The evangelist had taped a real ten-dollar bill to the back of the picture, which would have become the property of the child who asked about Jesus. The picture of Jesus was the most valuable item on the table, but no one even picked it up. No one even asked about it. The most valuable item was free for the asking.

Too often, adults are just like these children. We get motivated when we have the opportunity to earn money to purchase toys. Our toys simply get bigger as we get older: a truck, a boat, a four-wheeler, a diamond, land, new furniture, a pool, a computer; the list is endless. What's wrong with these things? Nothing. But when Jesus is passed over in our pursuit of them, we have broken the first commandment: "You shall have no other gods before me" (Exodus 20:3).

Today you will likely trade your time for money. You will then trade your money for things. If this is our primary goal, we simply trade our life for things. As you make your way through the store of life and view the many items for which you will give your money or your time, I remind you that Jesus is far more valuable than silver or gold. Jesus is more valuable than any person you are living to please or impress. Jesus is more valuable than your career. Jesus is more valuable than success. Jesus is more valuable than your hobbies. Will you make the same mistake as the children, who shopped with play money by choosing goods from the world, while forgetting about the best good of all—the Good News of Jesus Christ?

One reason that Advent is such an important time of the year is that it gives us more than three weeks to prepare for Jesus' birthday. Of course, we need that kind of time to get all of our shopping done, right? We are bombarded with the pressure to purchase gifts even before Thanksgiving. I usually have all my shopping done by Thanksgiving to avoid the mounting stress I feel as Christmas Day approaches and to focus more on the spiritual aspects of the season.

I wonder how often Jesus' birthday comes and goes for many Christians without one thought being given to the significance of the day because all thoughts of Jesus have been pushed out by the opening of presents, the coming and going of company, and the preparation of meals. All of these are good and necessary, but they must not usurp what's more important, worshiping Jesus.

It's so easy for adults to make the same mistake as the children who were choosing items at that revival setting. With all the wonderful items to choose from during the Advent season and then on Christmas Day, it's easy to overlook Jesus, even though it's His birthday we are celebrating.

Should we get into the habit of overlooking Jesus' First Coming, how can we prepare ourselves adequately for Jesus' Second Coming? The baby, who first came to us in a humble cattle stall, will come to us the second time from the clouds announced with trumpet blasts. We may overlook Him now if we choose, but it will be impossible to overlook Him during His Second Advent. Either He will find us ready or He will find us busy attending to all the other choices of life we've elevated before Him through the years.

Advent is important each year because it focuses our attention on Jesus' coming. There should be evidence in our lifestyles that we are giving our attention to the reason why He came. We come to understand that through Jesus, there is a free gift of God available to us, the gift of eternal life. It doesn't cost us anything. It is true Jesus demands obedience, but to receive Jesus we can do no better than to open our hearts and invite Him in—just as we are.

So, in the midst of the wares laid before you today, I want you to see this picture of Jesus: "Here I am! I stand at the door and knock. If anyone hears my voice and opens the door, I will come in and eat with him, and he with me" (Revelation 3:19-20). That picture's worth more than a thousand words. Jesus felt it was worth His life. What's it worth to you? Not very much if we look past Jesus and try to find our way by focusing on acquiring the things of this world. Don't look past Jesus. Remember Jesus on His birthday, and live each day as a gift to Him. If you do, you will have found your way.

Advent Actions

1. This takes a bit of work, but you never know how an effort like this will affect someone's life. Go to the website Pictures of Jesus 4 You Art Gallery/Store. (Find the link at www.thefaithlab.com/advent.) This website has about 300 different images of Jesus. They are copyright protected, so in order to use them, they must be purchased. Consider purchasing some inexpensive small photographs of Jesus and using the photographs along with your tip money at restaurants as witnessing tools. Attach a note with your gift. You might even give away a copy of this Advent book. Along with your tip, leave a copy of this book and say, "Merry Christmas." It's one gift that will not be forgotten, and you never know the powerful effect it might have on the recipient.

2. Give away the gift of yourself. Since Christmas is the celebration of God giving away Himself, we can capture a bit of God's example by giving ourselves away to those we love by making up a book of coupons redeemable for things like "an uninterrupted day (cell phones included) with me," "movie night with me," "campout night with me," "cookie baking day with me," "trip to the zoo day with me," etc. The gift here is the gift of time with you and the gift of memory building.

Prayer

God of Many Faces,

Did we overlook You today as Your disciples sometimes did? When You pointed it out to them, they were puzzled. You told them You were hungry and thirsty, but they did not feed You or give You drink. You told them You were naked, but they didn't clothe You, sick, but they didn't provide You with medicine, and in prison, but they didn't come to visit You. They couldn't remember any of this, Lord, so they asked when they overlooked You. You told them that whenever they saw others with these problems and helped them, they were actually helping You (Matthew 25:45).

Lord, we confess, we don't always see You in the poor. We see people who didn't go to school and didn't work very hard, and we see people who made a bed for themselves. Instead of seeing the hungry, we see people who had rather use their money to buy cigarettes than eat. Instead of seeing the sick, we see people who chose to squander their money rather than purchase insurance. Instead of seeing people in prison, we see people who are getting what they deserve. Are we missing something, Lord?

I know the poor, sick, hungry, and those in prison in Your day were often people who were mistreated and in trouble because of no fault of their own. There was little or no justice. Even so, if we spend our time playing judge, are we missing You? Help us to remember that we are a part of Your Kingdom, not because we deserve to be, but because of Your grace. Grant us the love to extend that grace among the least of these. Amen.

Spinning Rims Are a Sign of the Times
December 18

I was in Panama City Beach, Florida the first time I saw a car with a set of spinning rims. At first, I thought my eyes were playing tricks on me. The car was stopped, but it looked like the wheels were still moving.

Not long after that I saw an ad for spinning rims that read:

Pick up a set of spinning rims, bolt them on your car rims, and be the talk of the town. Spinning rims are simply a stunning add-on to your car, truck, or SUV. A handful of select individuals have this product. Join this elite group.

Spinning rims are a sign of the times. We live in a society that values motion and speed. Speed is important in industry. Cost is reduced and profits rise when products can be produced with speed. Speed is a major factor in sports. I cannot even think of a sport where slowness is valued. A selling point for Internet services is the speed at which they can deliver information to one's computer.

The majority of our restaurants stay in business because they meet the customers' demand that meals be served within a short period of time. Airlines that experience more than average delays greatly diminish their market ability because people do not like to wait or have their schedules altered.

Life is fast-paced. It has become like one long, moving

sidewalk. We seem to be in constant motion. Even when we sit still, it's like we are in motion. We often discover that when our bodies cease moving, our minds continue in motion. We toss and turn through the night. Our minds take us through exhausting dreams. We wake, but we aren't rested. Day in and day out, this kind of pattern takes its toll on our minds, our bodies, and our spirits. If we are in constant motion, we can become physically sick, emotionally fragile, socially irritable, mentally deficient, and spiritually bankrupt.

In 2004, the country music band Alabama embarked on its American Farewell Tour. The band has more than thirty number one country hits. In one of their hits, "I'm in a Hurry," they question this American trait of ours to stay in a hurry. The group sings:

> I hear a voice
> It says I'm running behind
> I better pick up my pace
> It's a race
> and there ain't no room for someone in second place.

Then the chorus:

> I'm in a hurry to get things done
> (oh,) I rush and rush until life's no fun
> All I really gotta do is live and die
> But, I'm in a hurry and don't know why.

The end of the year feels as if it accelerates with each passing day. The closer to Christmas Day we get, the faster life seems to travel. There's more to do with less time to get it done. We feel the stress mounting. Some people even dread the coming of this season because there's so much to do. Guests can be wonderful, but preparing for guests can also be exhausting.

It's ironic that all of this is wrapped around Jesus' birthday, but many can't be still long enough to reflect on their relationship with Jesus. Of course, the fact that you are reading this says a lot about your desire to be different this year.

The Psalmist said:

> *Come, behold the works of the LORD, how he has wrought desolations in the earth. He makes wars cease to the end of the earth; he breaks the bow, and shatters the spear, he burns the chariots with fire! 'Be still, and know that I am God. I am exalted among the nations, I am exalted in the earth!' The LORD of hosts is with us; the God of Jacob is our refuge (Psalm 46:8-11 RSV).*

The passage tells us that unless we pause and focus our hearts and minds on God, we will fail to see what God is doing around us. We will not understand what God desires to do within us. We will fail to acknowledge God's power and His sovereignty over us and this world.

John's gospel tells us that at the height of Jesus' popularity, when He "perceived that they were about to come and take Him by force to make Him king, He departed again to the mountain by Himself alone" (John 6:15 NKJV). Jesus left the fast pace of His ministry, slowing down long enough to get completely still. From the mountain of solitude, Jesus could see the big picture more clearly, so when He came down from the mountain, He knew which direction to walk.

Jesus could have easily gotten caught up in the urgency of the people, with their desire to be freed from Roman rule, with their desire to see the Kingdom of God as it was in the days of King David. Jesus maintained a proper balance and perspective by withdrawing to the mountains.

Jesus shows us by his life that it's not people whose lives that are in constant motion who belong to an elite group. Look closely. Many people allow their lives to become so packed with "busyness," even with good and important things, that there is no time left for God. When their lives spin out of control, they are left dazed and confused. The ad I quoted about spinners is simply wrong in what it says. Those who buy spinners are not in an elite group.

The wisdom of the Psalmist needs to sink deep into our souls and become a part of how we frame each day. We need to find time to be still, listen to the Lord, and allow the Lord to direct our paths. One of the secrets to an abundant life is to value and protect our time alone with God. This time alone is imperative if we are going to find our way through Advent or through any holy season.

The elite group is not the one that stays in constant motion. The group that God blesses is the one that finds time to be still and to ponder the Lord's call and direction, like Mary, who "kept all these sayings, pondering them in her heart" (Luke 2:19).

Advent Actions

1. Continue to allow God to direct your paths today. Today, as you pray, don't speak to God, at least not at first; just listen. For ten minutes, just sit still in a quiet, peaceful place and meditate. Pay attention to what God brings to your mind. Keep a note pad and pen handy. Jot down a few short notes to review later.

2. Either today or tomorrow, schedule two-minute to four-minute breaks, three or four times during the day, just to sit still and listen to God. If you have an alarm on your clock, phone, or computer, set the alarm as a reminder.

Prayer

God of Movement and Stillness,

We need You to pour Your blessings in our cups, but during this time of the year, we are so busy buying more cups, or filling up the ones we have, that we are not still long enough for you to pour anything in them. It's a busy time, Lord. You understand, don't You, if we don't have any time for You until the Christmas Eve service?

I didn't think so. That's why I am inviting You to walk with us as we use this Advent book to help us find our way through this season, Lord. Like the Magi who sought the Christ Child on that first Christmas, we are being intentional about seeking You now. So, we still our hearts and ask You to speak to us. Bring a calmness into our Spirit. Bring assurance to our steps. Help us to find our way to stillness in a world that's constantly in motion. Amen.

B-I-N-G-O
and
L-O-V-E
December 19

"B-42. I-15. O-9." The letters and numbers came through loudly over the amplification system as the women placed large red chips over the corresponding numbers on their bingo cards. At the end of the table, an Alzheimer's patient sat quietly in her wheelchair. Since she was unable to play her own card, her sitter played the card for her while attempting to carry on some conversation.

Down the table one of the residents of the nursing home used a large magnifying glass to help her see the numbers on her card. The stakes were not high—a one-dollar bill to the winner.

Make no mistake, though. These ladies don't compete against one another. They compete against themselves, seeking to overcome the maladies of each day. Making it out of the bed, down the hall, and to the bingo table is a victory. The game itself is a celebration. One lady, too feeble to sit at the table, reclines in a semi-fetal position near the others. Her victory is just being with the group.

"G-33." One lady overlooks that number on her card. The lady next to her notices and takes one of her chips and covers the number. Friend helping friend is the name of this game. As the game continues, the caller has to leave the room a couple of times, momentarily stopping play. The ladies show their virtue of patience, learned from having to wait upon others to help them with the daily necessities of life most of us take for granted. Waiting for a game to resume is a pleasant wait compared to waiting for someone to help you to the bathroom, to move you from your wheelchair into a bed, or to help manage your pain.

This community of nursing home residents is almost totally dependent upon others. They will live their lives out within the walls of the nursing home. They cannot leave on their own to have any of their needs met. They must wait for others to bring them what they need or they must create it for themselves as best they can. For those of us who are able bodied and relatively young, this place seems depressing. But to the residents, this place is home. It's not like the home they left and never will be, but it is home nonetheless. They share their home with other elderly people and with the workers, who give them care each day.

"N-11." In walks a member of the staff. He's a black man who looks to be in his late thirties. He sees one of the residents for whom he's developed a fondness. He leans down and gives the white woman a kiss on the cheek. "Thought I'd forgotten you, today, didn't you?" he asks. The woman forgets her bingo game momentarily. Her big smile reveals no teeth, but lots of joy. The man is about to go out the door, but turns back at the last moment, hugs another resident, and plants a big kiss on her cheek. Her black skin refuses to show a blush, but her demeanor gives the emotion away. She smiles and continues to play.

"O-40." A few minutes later this same lady "bingos." She doesn't yell the word "bingo," as most winners do. In fact, her neighbors seem more excited than she does about her good fortune, and they draw the attention of the caller. Perhaps her tempered excitement has to do with the prize being a single dollar. Or perhaps the love and affection from an orderly was the prize she had been waiting for. Love is worth living for. Residents in our nursing homes wait for our love, and they wait to give their love away. No longer can they leave their home to give their love away or to receive the love they need in order to live. They wait for people like you and me to remind them of their worth.

President George W. Bush in his inaugural address said that every day each of us is called upon to do small things with great love. I thought of that orderly at the nursing home, hugging and kissing those elderly ladies. I thought of the sitter who played the bingo card for the lady with Alzheimer's, giving her constant attention. I thought about the middle-aged woman who awaited the return of her bedridden mother from the hospital. I thought about the resident who leaned over to help her friend by placing a chip on a missed number. When we do small things with great love, it communicates to others that the love of God is within us. When we place the chips of our day on L-O-V-E, regardless of how small the action may be or seem, we've scored a "bingo" in the eyes of God.

During the fourth week of Advent, we are quickly approaching the day we celebrate the birth of Christ, God's gift of love to humanity. Two verses on love come to mind: The first is John 3:16: "For God so loved the world that he gave his one and only Son, that whoever believes in him shall not perish but have eternal life." The second one is John 15:13: "Greater love has no one than this, that he lay down his life for his friends."

One verse tells us that the reason Jesus came into the world was love, and the other verse tells us the reason Jesus died was love. Our very purpose in life is to love. First of all, we are to love the Lord our God with all our heart, and with all our soul, and with all our mind, and with all our strength. Secondly, we are to love our neighbor as we love ourselves (Mark 12:29-31).

Without love there would be no Advent. Jesus would have never come. For Advent to become real to others, the ministry of presence needs to occur. Nursing home residents need our presence. Homebound people need our presence. Those who are experiencing their first Christmas without a loved one need our presence. The people in prison need our presence. Those in drug rehabilitation need our presence. The unwed mother needs our presence. The teenager who just broke up with her boyfriend needs our presence. Those celebrating the birth of a child need our presence. Close friends need our presence. Family members need our presence. Those throwing a party to bring in the New Year need our presence.

Of course, we can't be everywhere. But love dictates that we invest in the lives of people. That's what Jesus did. That's what He came to do. If we love Jesus, that's what we will do, too.

Today, what small thing might you do with great love? If you need someone to show you the way, just travel down to the local nursing home. There the residents will show you and teach you just how important small gestures of love really are.

Advent Actions

1. Visit someone this week in a nursing home or retirement care facility. Call the activities director and find out what activities are taking place with the residents during the holidays and what ways you could best interact with them. Many of these residents are starving for attention, touch, conversation, and love.

2. Visit a homebound member. Speak with a minister about taking and serving Holy Communion to homebound members in your church. Homebound members are cut off from the church body and do not have the opportunity to participate in Holy Communion. Different faiths/denominations have different traditions/practices regarding the serving of the communion elements. Find out what is acceptable in your tradition. You might even be allowed to participate in the serving of this remembrance meal. It's powerful and meaningful to these precious members of the church. You might create a brief 10-minute service complete with a song, prayer and a two-to-five minute homily to go with the serving of the communion meal.

3. Think of one small thing you can do that represents your love of Christ. Do it for someone you know or do it for a stranger.

Prayer

God of Love,

You showed us the true meaning of love through Jesus. We praise You that through Jesus You emptied yourself; You poured out Yourself like a drink offering to show us the depth of Your love.

You have taught us that if we are to be Your disciples we need to emulate You. We confess that we are often selfish. When we have a chance to pour ourselves out for others, we hold back. We want to make sure there's enough left in the cup for us.

During Advent, help us to be more lavish with our love. In the name of the One who gave His only begotten Son, help us begin by doing some small things so great things might happen in the hearts of people we meet.

Give us eyes and ears that are attentive to the needs around us. Give us hearts that will fill with compassion to meet their needs. Give us feet and hands that are busy with more than gift shopping, such as meeting the needs of those around us, especially the needs of the lonely, the elderly, the poor, and those who may have been forgotten by others during Advent. Amen.

All Is Calm?
December 20

Joseph Mohr imagined that the first Christmas was still and peaceful. "All is calm," writes Mohr in his song, "Silent Night." Even though the baby Jesus seems to be born at night, Mohr writes that "all is bright," that "darkness flies, all is light." And though the night is silent, angels can be heard singing, "Alleluia! Hail the King!" It's subtle, but Mohr juxtaposes the darkness with light and the silence with sound. The radiant beams from the face of the Holy One are brighter because of the darkness into which He is born. The angels' chorus is more pronounced as it breaks the silence of the night.

The song is one of the more beautiful hymns of the season. But it leaves me wondering if the words are realistic. Was it a calm night? It was a long journey, perhaps on the back of a donkey, and brought the realization upon arriving in Bethlehem that there was not even an empty room for a pregnant woman about to give birth. What kind of calm is that?

What I hear breaking the silence of the night are the screams of a woman pushing a baby into the world—the crying of a newborn baby. What I hear are the scurrying feet of a nervous father, who may have had to deliver this child. What I hear are the sounds of animals that have been displaced from their normal sleeping quarters to make room for this couple, temporarily homeless, and for their newborn child. I don't hear a lot of calm in this story, at least not initially.

I don't usually hear a lot of calm during Advent either. What I hear breaking the silence are the sounds of families in crises. I hear the scurrying feet of shoppers madly moving through stores looking for gifts. I hear children asking, "Are we there yet?" as they head to their grandmother's house. I hear traffic, honking horns, jingling bells that never stop, commercials, and demands for deadlines, for unless the work is done, there can be no fun during the holidays. I hear the poor asking for food and gifts for their kids.

Calmness is elusive. One Sunday during Advent, right in the middle of my sermon, just as I was about to move to an important point, I heard music. It was faint, but distinct. It was a Christmas carol, but the tune never registered with me. The sound rattled me. I knew I should ignore it, move on, pretend I didn't hear it. But my words began to run together and pile up, like a derailed train. Finally, I stopped in mid-sermon and asked, "Where's that music coming from?" And perhaps for the first time in the sermon, everyone was listening. But what most people heard were my own anxieties over the distraction and not the faint beeping of a Christmas tune. I was anything but cool, calm, and collected. I later learned that it was coming from a computer chip in a man's tie that accidentally got pressed in the "on" position.

Little did I know that at the same time, my wife had been summoned by a member who thankfully had arrived late for church, informing her that the fire alarm was sounding in our home across the street. My wife arrived to discover that our noon meal had burned on the stove and in time to keep the alarm company from dispatching the fire truck to our residence. If I could not preach through an electronic Christmas carol, I know I couldn't have preached through the sounds of a fire truck arriving in front of the church. All is calm?

One Advent, in my hometown of Louisville, Alabama, the calmness of a Saturday evening was broken with the siren sounding from downtown. In my hometown, the siren was the signal for the volunteer firefighters to gather at the fire station. The police on duty would give the first two volunteers the location of the fire, and they would jump in the fire truck and head off to the fire. Others would follow.

It was unseasonably cold that weekend in South Alabama. The temperature had dropped into the teens. To keep the water in the fire truck from freezing, someone had placed a portable propane heater inside the garage where the fire truck was parked. The first two responders didn't know that. As they drove out of the garage, they ran over the propane tank and it exploded, catching all the hoses on the truck on fire. The fire truck then sat in the middle of the street ablaze, along with the wooden garage where the fire truck was parked. Volunteer fire departments from Clio, Clayton, and Bakerhill all responded as the blaze threatened the fireworks store that was in the same building where the fire truck had been parked. A gas station was momentarily threatened next door. It was so cold water was freezing in the street as they put out the blaze.

Life can go from calm to chaos in a matter of minutes.

Here's a thought: we would not know, understand, or appreciate calmness were it not for the comedy and the tragedy of errors and chaos in life. I do believe there was a calmness that came to Joseph and Mary after the birth of Jesus. It was the same calmness that most couples feel after a newborn has been safely delivered, placed in a mother's arms, and later a father's, as they meet face to face for the first time.

If this Advent season is like all others, there will be some chaos in your life. Initially, the season may not resemble the unmistakable calm of a freshly fallen snow. But somewhere in the midst of the season, that moment will come. It may happen after the company has returned home. It may happen after the children have opened their gifts. It may happen after you have visited the grave of a loved one. It may happen after you have returned home from a vacation.

It may happen after you have attended a Christmas Eve communion service. It may happen after you have visited an elderly person in a nursing home. It may happen after you've sat still, alone, and prayed. It may happen at a gathering of friends. When the moment comes, it may take you by surprise, but when it does, you will know that you have found your way through an important part of this Advent season.

Advent Actions

1. Because the practice of meditation has long been associated with Eastern religion, many Christians have shied away from the benefits it offers. We don't have to embrace Eastern religion to be in touch with our body, mind, and spirit. It's no more sinful to learn to calm ourselves and think more clearly in stressful situations from a Hindu than it is to learn physics from a Muslim, so don't get uptight with this Advent action.

One of the world's simplest and most effective methods for calming yourself and making yourself feel stronger is based on an ancient Hindu technique that doesn't need any special equipment—only your hands; you can do it any time, anywhere.

If you feel anxious, weak, scattered, tense, or out of control, this will help you to feel more solid and grounded. This technique is especially helpful for people with breathing problems, but all of us will feel calmer and stronger when we try it.

A. Sit in a comfortable posture and begin to meditate on your breath. As you meditate, pay attention to how relatively deep or shallow your breathing is, but don't try to change its movement.

B. Once you're in touch with the movements of your breath, make a fist with each of your hands by closing your fingers loosely over your thumbs. Then, still watching your breath, squeeze your thumbs firmly with one steady pressure and hold it for a minute or so.

C. As soon as you squeeze your thumbs, your breathing will become markedly deeper and stronger. If you study the changes that take place in your feelings, you'll discover that along with the new feelings of strength in your breathing, you also feel more solid and grounded in both your mind and your body.

D. The harder you squeeze your thumbs, the deeper your breathing will become and the more solid and strong you'll feel at every level of being.

E. Release your thumbs and allow your breathing to return to its original state. Once you've released the pressure on your thumbs, notice how relatively weak and shallow your "normal" way of breathing feels compared to the way it felt while you were squeezing your thumbs.[14]

2. Each day for the remainder of Advent and thereafter, get into the habit of claiming a few calming moments each day. Discover what calms you: a cup of coffee, a favorite CD, a bubble bath, the aroma of a burning candle, soft light, finding something to laugh about, exercise, prayer, reading a devotional, or writing in a journal. Give yourself permission each day to spend some time doing something that brings a sense of calm to your chaos. A ten-minute time-out may grant you the springboard you need to continue giving both quality and quantity of time to others that's required of you.

Prayer

God Incarnate, Who Spoke and Calmed the Sea,

There's a tempest within our souls and we can't find the harbor. Be our lighthouse. Shine Your light brightly for us. Guide us away from the rocks. We are restless and weary. While the storm may continue to rage, grant us a calmness within. Give us the assurance that we will step foot on solid ground without running aground.

Help us to hear Your voice over the competing voices of this world. May Your voice be clear and distinguishable from all the others. Just as the sea grew calm at the command of Jesus' voice, may our souls find a calmness at the sound of the Your voice. Speak to us, Lord. Speak to us clearly this Advent. Break through all that's not calm. Show us how to set aside life's chaos, long enough to create moments of calm and feel the peace of the Christ Child. Amen.

We Can Have Joy
in the Winters of Life
December 21

In the children's book, *The Tree that Survived the Winter*, a tree realizes it has survived the hardships of winter.

> *Her roots seemed to be extending further and more firmly into the soil. Her arms seemed to embrace more of the world, not with the timid gestures of a sapling afraid of tangling with the wind, but with the freedom of knowing that the wind could not topple her. 'I have survived the winter,' she marveled aloud.*[15]

Advent comes in the midst of winter, and for some people the season is less than joyful. It's a season of winter for their souls. Unlike the tree of the children's book, they've not yet made it through to the other side. While everyone around them seems to be singing "Joy to the World," all they want to do is pull the shades and close out the world.

What was the Apostle Paul thinking when he wrote to the church of Thessalonica, "Be joyful always"? Was he from another planet? Didn't he ever have a bad day? Didn't he know pain? Didn't he understand suffering, grief, disappointment, and discouragement? Well, as a matter of fact, he did.

To the church at Corinth Paul wrote:

> *Five times I received from the Jews the forty lashes minus one. Three times I was beaten with rods, once*

I was stoned, three times I was shipwrecked, I spent a night and a day in the open sea, I have been constantly on the move. I have been in danger from rivers, in danger from bandits, in danger from my own countrymen, in danger from Gentiles; in danger in the city, in danger in the country, in danger at sea; and in danger from false brothers. I have labored and toiled and have often gone without sleep; I have known hunger and thirst and have often gone without food; I have been cold and naked. Besides everything else, I face daily the pressure of my concern for all the churches (2 Corinthians 11:24-28).

Okay, so Paul had been dipped in the fire, but he can't be saying that a person is supposed to remain joyful through stuff like this, can he?

Here's what I believe Paul teaches us. The joy we have in Jesus transcends circumstances. Circumstances can produce happy moments as well as sad moments and times of grief. However, Christians cannot allow circumstances to become the dominant factor that determines whether we have joy.

Many people look for joy during Christmas in the lights, the shopping, the decorating, the cooking, the family, the gifts, and the football games. These things bring only temporary joy. The pleasure comes and then it's gone. The buildup may have taken weeks or months, and then it is over in minutes or hours. There's a letdown and you aren't sure why. Lasting joy has depth that penetrates deeper than the season, deeper than the event, and deeper than any gift. Lasting joy is connected to Christ himself.

When studying those occasions in the New Testament where joy is mentioned, I found that the passages hover over and around the gift of Christ, much as the Star of David hovered over the

Bethlehem stable all those years ago. In studying those passages, I came to realize that when the Apostle Paul said, "Be joyful always," he was referring to the foundation we have in Christ.

Because of this foundation, there are no circumstances that can take joy away from us. Every time a person in the New Testament refers to joy, that individual refers to a joy that goes deep, a joy that is embodied in the personhood and deity of Christ, or a joy that a person has in relation to Christ. It's a joy that cannot be taken away regardless of the circumstances that come our way.

Does this mean we are never sad, never depressed, that we never grieve, hurt, or despair? Not at all. The birth of Christ was a gift of joy to the world, a gift to Mary and to Joseph. Yet the gospel writers never paint for us a picture of a blissful, painless, stress-free birth. Far from it. Ladies, does traveling nine months pregnant on a donkey over many miles to get to a small town with no vacant rooms sound painless and stress free?

What about Matthew's account of Jesus' family having to flee into Egypt in fear of being killed by King Herod? Only Matthew records the gruesome "Flight into Egypt," which links Advent with the death of many innocent babies killed because Herod was jealous of the news of a baby king. There was no joy for those mothers and fathers.

James I. Cook, in an article titled "Joy to the World/Pain in the World," expresses his gratitude to Matthew for including the story of the massacre of the innocent children in his Christmas account. He wrote:

> *I turn to it again and again, when someone I know loses a loved one at the height of the Christmas season. It helps me—and I hope it helps them—to remember that theirs are not the first tears to fall on Christmas; to recall that there has never been a Christmas of pure*

peace and happiness; that 'joy to the world' has always been sung to the accompaniment of much 'pain in the world.' [16]

Part of the miracle of Christmas is that "Joy to the World" is sung at all because it is never sung in the absence of pain and suffering. But it is sung. For some, it is a song of hope. For some, it is hope that joy will return. For others, it is a song of confession that through Christ joy is here already and that joy will continue to come because Christ will continue to come and break through all that is wrong, painful, and sad in this world of ours.

Right now it is still winter on the calendar. For some, it is winter in their hearts. Like the first settlers that came to this country who had to learn to sustain the harsh winters in order to get to the beautiful springs and the lush summers, our joy can be magnified when we learn to look beyond the hardships of the winter and know that spring is coming. We must maintain faith that God is at work during the difficult days, preparing us for the dawn of better ones.

The season of Advent prepares us for Christmas Day, the day that Joy came down from heaven and entered into the hardships of humanity as a vulnerable child. He became our high priest, one able "to sympathize with our weaknesses" because He "has been tempted in every way, just as we are —yet was without sin" (Heb. 4:15).

Wherever you are in your journey today, remember the promise of Jesus, "And surely I am with you always, to the very end of the age" (Matthew 28:20). That's why He has the name "Immanuel." That's why we can have joy, even in the winters of life.

Advent Actions

1. Look back over the year and write down the names of those who have lost loved ones. Remember, this will be their first Christmas without that person. Send them a note that acknowledges their grief, while emphasizing the hope we still have in Jesus.

2. Go to the library and check out the book, *The Tree that Survived the Winter*. If you have a child or a grandchild, you've got a good excuse. Read the book and think about the metaphors for the winters of your life.

Prayer

God of All Seasons,

Thank You that You are present during the dormant seasons of life. It's easy to praise You when warm breezes blow, when the rain falls gently to the earth and there is ample shade from the heat of the day. When the seasons of life change and dormant times like grief, loneliness, hardship, despair, pain, anxiety, uncertainty, doubt, loss, addiction, and depression sweep over our lives, we admit that praise doesn't come so easily. Joy is harder to find. But God of All Seasons, we have discovered that joy during times like these is not surface level. It's more like an underground stream. It's a joy that runs deep.

During the dormant seasons of life, You are faithful. You remind us to pull our joy from a deeper well, from a deeper source. We thank You, Lord, that our joy isn't contingent on circumstances, but is based on a God who gives joy in all seasons. While the seasons of life change, Lord, You never do. You are constant. That is why even in the midst of tragedy we are able to say, "It is well, it is well with our souls." God of All Seasons, we praise You! Amen.

Herod Launched the First War on Christmas and He Lost
December 22

A few years ago, I was travelling from Georgia to Alabama and came through Abbeville, a small town on Highway 10, just across the Alabama/Georgia state line. I noticed the Christmas decorations on the city streets. The banners that hung from the poles read "Holiday Greetings."

These decorations didn't look new. I doubt the city council recently put them up to be politically correct. They are likely the same decorations the city has had for years. But they caught my attention because of the "war on Christmas" we've heard so much about.

These decorations, of course, are completely appropriate. They are up from Thanksgiving until after New Year's Day. "Holiday Greetings" encompasses the entire season. I wouldn't have given these banners a second thought had there not been so much made of whether it's appropriate to say "Merry Christmas," or whether we should whitewash "Christmas" from our vocabulary in an effort to be inoffensive to those of other religions.

The media have fanned this issue into a blaze to have something to debate on their networks. Many evangelical pastors have rallied their Christian supporters around this issue and during a season that's supposed to be full of Christmas cheer, many Christians are hopping mad, afraid that people are trying to stomp out Christmas.

Even President Bush was brought into the fray. Although

cards have been going out of the White House for over a decade with a "Holiday Greeting" message rather than a "Merry Christmas," because of the media attention over this issue, President Bush "caught heat" from Christian conservatives saying he had bowed to liberals and was afraid to stand up for his Christian beliefs.

But is there another side to this issue? Let's say Joe Lieberman runs for the Presidency in 2016 and wins. Now that's not likely, but this is America. What kind of card would you expect President Lieberman to send out? Do you think Christians would be offended if he were to send a card that read "Happy Hanukkah"? Do you think such a card would be received with good cheer? Hardly. Unless, of course, you happen to be Jewish. I wonder what kind of cards his constituents in Connecticut receive.

Christians throughout the land would protest that an American President was trying to impose his religious holiday upon them. Would those of other faiths feel the same way should they receive a card from the President with a Christian message? Remember, it's not like the President is really sending out a personal greeting. Cards are being sent with the Presidential seal and paid for with taxpayers' money. Herein is the problem. Such a card at least gives the appearance that government is supporting one religion over another, and the First Amendment clearly prohibits that.

As long as Christians are in the majority, we don't want to see these issues from the perspective of those in the minority. But we need only review our history to be reminded that this country was founded by those seeking religious liberty, people who were once in the minority. Ironically, those who came to these American shores seeking religious liberty did not grant religious liberty to those who settled here.

Strangely enough, there was even a time in the history of our country when it was the Christians who banned the celebration of Christmas. Puritans who immigrated to Massachusetts disliked Christmas because it reminded them of the Church of England and the customs of the old world. Because the date of December 25 wasn't selected as the date of Christ's birth until several centuries after the death of Christ, the Puritans didn't place any trust in the date. The holiday was frowned upon by the Puritans because people of the lower class visited wealthier families and begged, and in some cases demanded food and drink in return for toasts to their host's health in a practice called "wassailing." The ban on Christmas existed as law in Massachusetts for 22 years, and the disapproval of Christmas celebrations in the Boston region extended into the mid-1800s.[17]

It took Baptists like Roger Williams and Obadiah Holmes to stand up for religious freedom, for freedom to disagree with the religion of the majority and even for the freedom of those who chose not to believe in God at all.

America is the most ethnically and religiously diverse nation on the planet. While Christmas Day will always be Christmas Day for Christians, and the real significance of this day for us is found in the manger of Bethlehem, we should seek to understand and respect those whose religious faith differs from our own.

I'm not suggesting that we remove every vestige of the sacred nature of the season for the benefit of those who do not worship as we do; quite the contrary. As individual Christians, we should take every opportunity to emphasize the true meaning of this season. We need to extend the message of Christmas among nonbelievers and to those who need to be shown the love of Jesus and who need to understand the spirit of Christmas through our actions and our greetings.

However, where the public must be embraced and the masses welcomed, we should not get too bent out of shape if the official policy of a company or the government is to use the phrase "Happy Holidays." Besides, a non-believer is just as likely to say "Merry

Christmas" as a Christian and not think anything about its meaning. In doing so, saying "Merry Christmas" becomes a nonreligious phrase.

Since when has saying "Merry Christmas" to people changed their lives anyway? Lives are changed by loving people as Jesus commanded. Carrying Christmas to people via the Christ Child changes lives. That love first showed up in the vulnerable package of a babe wrapped in swaddling clothes in Bethlehem.

When King Herod found out about the birth of this King, he sought to have the child killed. Yes, the war on Christmas has been going on for quite a long time. Those who tried to stomp it out marred the very first Christmas.

This dragnet of death was designed to get rid of this boy king and kill Christmas. All those efforts failed. Is our faith so shallow that we are afraid that Christmas is in danger because department store workers are told to wish people "Holiday Greetings" instead of a "Merry Christmas"? Since when did we give this sacred season to the retailers anyway? Hmmm. Now that's a good question.

Christians shouldn't worry about the efforts of others to kill Christmas if we allow Christ to live within us and through us, if we seek to spread the love of Christ to others, if we do our job and witness about our Lord while respecting the beliefs of others. As long as we worship the baby born in the manger, who eventually leads us to the man who bled on the cross for the remission of our sins; as long as we stoop down and peer into the empty tomb and believe that the chains of death could not hold Jesus; as long as we embrace the continuing presence of the Holy Spirit in our lives and do as that Christmas song entreats us to do, "Go tell it on the mountain!" Christmas will always be alive and the world will always know it. Merry Christmas!

Advent Actions

1. If you really want to get someone's attention and emphasize Christ, try saying "Merry CHRISTmas." That'll get your point across.

2. Before you become too critical of the secular trying to take over the sacred traditions of the season, do a little research and you'll discover that Christians did the opposite in our early history. Some of the Christmas traditions we now celebrate were taken from secular/ pagan traditions. Perhaps the biggest example is the date of Christmas itself, December 25. How did we arrive at that date? Google it, or read the history of Advent at the end of the book.

3. Take inventory of your traditions. Do you take every opportunity to emphasize the true meaning of Christmas? Christmas Day is the day we celebrate the birthday of Jesus. How many Christians actually do anything religious on Christmas Day? What about you?

Prayer

Merry Christmas, God,

That sounds a bit odd to give You such a greeting. I kind of doubt You get caught up in the marking of the day we celebrate as the birth of Your son. We are told we don't have the date correct. We wonder, if we were to celebrate the day as You would have us, what would it look like, Lord? Would You have us handing out gold or just obeying the golden rule: "So in everything, do to others what you would have them do to you" (Matthew 7:13)?

Lord, what if we started saying "Merry Christmas" to people in July? That would certainly get people's attention. Maybe it's a good sign, Lord, that there's at least some debate about the "Happy Holidays" versus the "Merry Christmas" greeting. But, Lord, help us not lose focus of the larger issue, which isn't whether this greeting is indicative that secular society is becoming less tolerant of Christians, but whether Christians are becoming less intentional to emphasize the Christian story in places where we should. Forgive us, Lord, of becoming too secular within our own space. Remind us that before we can win a battle for the souls of others, we must first get our souls in line with You. Amen.

Now I Remember Why I Bought the Boat
December 23

Pat Greenwell, diving coach for the University of Alabama, never lets a diving meet pass in Moultrie, Georgia without getting in a little bit of fishing in some of Colquitt County's ponds. For years I envied his Gheenoe, which he pulled behind his truck from Tuscaloosa.

A Gheenoe is best described as a cross between a canoe and a Jon boat. You can put a Gheenoe in small rivers and ponds, and it is also great for fishing the saltwater flats. Equip the boat with a trolling motor, and you can ease up on a bass sleeping behind a log. Put a 16-horsepower motor behind her, and it'll push you upstream like a knife cutting through hot butter.

I shopped around and finally bought one of my own. Although I love fishing, I purchased the boat for one main reason—to spend more time with my teenage sons. The first time I took my son Ryan fishing in the Gheenoe, he caught a seven-pound bass! I thought, "Man, it doesn't get any better than this! Memories! Good times!"

My boys have grown up now; they've moved away. As I said, they were the real reason I bought the Gheenoe. It never was about me. I love to fish but I've never been in love with the boat. I've never taken her out, launched her, told her how much I loved her, and what a great team we make. "I've never caught a bass, held it up, showed it to her, and thanked her for making it all possible. The Gheenoe's a two-seater and unless the other seat is occupied, she's incomplete. Now that my sons have moved away, the boat's not used very much.

Occasionally other people fill the seat, friends from church, or friends from out of town. You can get in a lot of good talking out on a boat in between casts.

Mostly, my boat is like boats most people own. She just sits and waits, sits and waits, and waits some more. On 75-degree days when there's no wind, if she could make animal noises, she would whine like a dog if you walked right past her and didn't hook her up to the truck. On 80-degree days she would bark a time or two. On 85-degree days, she wouldn't stop barking. You'd have to go out and hose her down to make her be quiet.

My boat has sat and waited so long, sometimes for months that I've thought about finding her a new owner. I've heard that the two happiest days in a boat owner's life are the day he buys a boat and the day he sells it. I say "he" because owning a boat is mostly a "he" thing. I don't know many women who own boats. In fact, I don't know any.

When we lived in South Georgia, the temperature would climb high enough during the Christmas holidays to do some occasional fishing. One year, when my younger son had already gone back to the University of Tennessee to prepare for a big diving competition, my older son and I had a few more days together. The weather climbed into the mid-sixties, and even though the Gheenoe doesn't whine that much on windy days in the mid-sixties, it was a rare opportunity to do a little fishing with my son, John. We made plans to launch the boat. A county farmer gave us permission to fish his pond. He wanted John to know that his service to our country as a Marine was appreciated.

I bought the boat because I knew that it's difficult for father and son to escape each other while they are on a boat. For a small period of time, they cannot escape each other unless one wants to take a swim. Usually, you are guaranteed at least one great moment; if not a big fish, at least you might be able to talk about the one that got away. It's bonding time.

When I fished with my teenage sons, sometimes there was good conversation. In those days, I found that I was the one trying to make most of the conversation. I was the one trying to figure out what was going on in their lives. Teenagers are like combination locks. You are always trying to figure out the numbers that unlock their hearts and minds.

That day was different. I was no longer fishing with a boy. My son had become a man. I was fishing with Lance Corporal John Helms. That day I didn't have to turn the tumblers. All I had to do was listen. We fished the edges and the shallows, but our conversation was deeper than ever. I discovered that I'd raised a young man with more depth than I realized. His heart was open and his mind was clearer than I'd ever known it to be. He and I acknowledged some of the mistakes we'd made along the way in our relationship, but more than that, we embraced the goodness of our relationship and our love for one another.

I was working the trolling motor. I was guiding us around the pond, leading us to the places where we caught plenty of bass on a cool, windy day. I was where I'd always tried to be, in the guiding role. Though every father makes mistakes in raising his children, I tried with the help of my wife to lead and guide our children in the ways of the Lord as they grew up. As the proverb says, "Teach a child to choose the right path, and when he is older, he will remain upon it" (Proverbs 22:6 TLB).

The last bass John caught that day weighed five pounds. The bass came up and hit a jitterbug, a top-water lure. It's a great moment for a fisherman to see a bass bust a top-water plug. Greater still is the moment for a father to share honest and deep conversation with his children. Sharing some of the most meaningful conversation with my son I've ever had and seeing the joy on his face as he landed that bass, reminded me why I bought that boat and why I don't need to sell it.

Advent Actions

1. More than gifts under the tree, children long for and cherish bonding times with parents during Advent. Sometime during Advent make time to do something special with each of your children or grandchildren.

2. Take time to write about a special memory you have with your mother or father, son or daughter, or other significant person in your life, and include it in a card that you give or send to that person this Advent.

Prayer

God of Loving Memories,

When the Children of Israel crossed the Jordan River, You instructed them to take stones from the river and make an altar to worship You. You are a God of loving memories.

Many of us suffer from bad memories, Lord. We have pain from relationships that were not good, that could have been better, that were marked by some unfortunate circumstances. Like Forrest Gump's girlfriend Jenny, some of us are haunted by our memories and we can't find enough rocks to throw at them. We pray that you will allow the ocean to wash the waves upon those memories as it would a sand castle, little by little eroding them away. If it's not possible to forget, at least may they not hold power over us, Lord.

May they be replaced with other memories, new ones that we can build and create over the years with family and friends, ones that are peaceful, that are filled with laughter, joy, and warm affirmation, and that are more than a "flash in the pan," but a way of life. May life become a memory-building experience, made possible because You are in our midst, Lord.

With You among us during Advent, Lord, we can be assured that the season will produce something meaningful. You are the One guiding us, directing us, and showing us where to cast and where to drop anchor. You are the One teaching us to be fishers of men. Amen.

Rings of Fire
December 24

The cold wind could be felt pushing its way through the cracks of the oak wood floor. Sometimes it was brisk enough to flicker the flames that rose in the fireplace of the family room, Carrie Sue's favorite room.

Carrie Sue Reynolds, age ten, would sit for hours watching as whole logs were transformed into hot coals. The fire seemed to hypnotize her. She loved the fireplace so much that she even volunteered for a job nobody else in a family of seven wanted, taking out the ashes in the evening and starting up a new fire in the morning. Some nights she even curled up on a rug in front of the fire and slept until the next morning.

Being a light sleeper, she woke to the distant sound of the whistle from the steam locomotive of the Southern Railway Company that passed through Lula promptly at 6:00 a.m. Even in the summer when there was no fire to light, she would get up at the sound of the train whistle. Sometimes she even ran down to the crossing to watch as the train rolled by headed to other stops along its route: Gillsville, Maysville, Harmony Grove, Nicholson, Center, and Athens, places that seemed a world away for Carrie Sue, who rarely left home.

Carrie's brother Nathan did most of the wood chopping. He also brought the wood inside and stacked it on the hearth. He hated his job just as much as Carrie Sue loved hers. He was convinced if everybody in the family took a turn of chopping and toting wood they would stay a lot warmer and spend a lot less time complaining about the cold.

In the Reynolds family, complaining was as much a part of the family routine as milking the cows before the sun rose. The boys complained about having to share a bed. Carrie Sue complained about being the only girl. Their father complained about never having enough money to provide for his family, especially at Christmas. Their mother complained about having to listen to everyone complain.

Carrie Sue found out how important money was to the family the day she turned ten, which was just a week before Christmas. Her mother baked a birthday cake and threw a party outside under the oak tree. Carrie Sue and two of her friends took turns swinging on a tire swing her father had hung from the huge oak tree as her birthday present. In addition to the swing, Carrie's father gave her a shiny nickel. It was the first coin he'd ever given Carrie Sue.

The day after her birthday, Carrie Sue and her friend Beth were walking the railroad tracks looking for some of her pin creations. Her brother Justin had shown Carrie Sue how to place a couple of straight pins on the track in a crisscross pattern. The pressure of the train would press the pins together and make them look like a tiny pair of scissors. She had made other clever designs from the pins as well—a house, a stick man, and a bug—all magically transformed by the pressure of the train's steel rollers pressing on the rail.

As they placed more pins on the rail, Carrie Sue felt the nickel in the bottom of her pants pocket. The nickel could have purchased several sticks of licorice at Millard's Crossroads Store, but she was more interested in seeing what "that man's face" would look like after the train ran over it. She placed her nickel on the track and waited anxiously until the next morning. She got her nickel's worth of excitement when she ran to the tracks to find her nickel flattened to the size of a quarter. But her joy quickly turned to deep regret when she showed the coin to her father.

Her father Wayne yelled and screamed and told her how hard money was to come by and that she should have known better than to destroy it. He made her go out in the yard and break off a switch from the Chinaberry tree that grew by the back porch. Wayne Reynolds often carried his discipline too far, causing his children to have conflicted feelings; they loved him, but they were also very afraid of him, especially when he was drinking.

Carrie Sue's whipping had as much to do with her wasting the nickel as it did with how she wasted it. The railroad had once been a friend of her family, but her father was disabled from an accident that happened at work with the railroad. He had worked as a brakeman, a dangerous job that sometimes required him to ride on the top of moving freight cars. One day he slipped between the cars; and the train severed his leg. He was fortunate to have survived.

Instead of being grateful for life, Wayne lost his self-respect. He didn't feel like a man anymore. "When a man can't work," he'd often say to the family, "he ain't worth nothin'." The anger about the incident burned within him. The hot coals he kept in his gut were as real as those Carrie Sue stoked in the fireplace. Carrie Sue didn't understand all of that. She just knew that her daddy was mad about the flattened nickel and that her legs ached from the stripes he left on them.

Carrie Sue didn't understand why her father drank liquor, either. She and her brothers just knew that when he started drinking, they'd better stay out of his way. As poor as the Reynolds family was, Wayne always seemed to find enough money to purchase liquor. It was the only thing he'd found to escape the pain of his troubled soul.

Two days before Christmas, the temperature had dropped considerably. The family gathered in the family room to stay warm. Carrie Sue's mother, Virginia, sat in the rocking chair crocheting her last Christmas gift. She was a quiet woman, but strong. Even though she never stood her ground with her husband, she was the emotional stability for the family.

The children held their breath when they heard the 1924 Model T pickup roll into the yard. The closer it got to Christmas Day, the more their father drank. He usually stayed drunk from Christmas Eve until New Year's Day.

As he slammed the door of the truck, they heard him muttering something about the railroad. They heard his boot touch the first step, followed by the unique sound of his prosthesis hitting the next step, then the sounds of his uneven stride across the porch to the screen door. As he opened the door, he began hollering for Virginia. Carrie Sue hid under the bed. The boys put away their checkers and hid in the closet.

Wayne entered the house and yelled, "Virginia, where's my supper? You ain't cooked me no supper in two days." He walked into the family room. Virginia began putting away her crochet. "Wayne, we ate supper three hours ago," she said.

"You talking back to me, woman?" he asked.

"No, Wayne, it's just that I don't know when to have supper for you if I don't know when you are coming home."

With that response, Wayne slapped his wife. From under the bed Carrie Sue saw her mother drop to her knees. "Get up, woman! You ain't fit to be no one's wife," he said. He pulled her up by her hair and grabbed her hand. Feeling her wedding band in his hand, he placed his other hand on her wrist and twisted the band until it came off her finger. "You ain't fit to be no one's wife," he said again. Without any thought, he threw Virginia's wedding band into the hot fire. "And I ain't going to be married to no woman who don't cook me no damn supper."

With that, Wayne Reynolds took off his ring and threw it into the fire too, as he turned to walk out the door. From under the

bed Carrie Sue watched as the flames flickered from the wind cre-
ated by the draft as her father opened the door to leave the house.
He stumbled down the steps and out to his truck. He drove away as
Virginia cried, slumped over in her rocker.

The children came out of hiding and began to console their
mother. "Mommy, I know Daddy loves you," Carrie Sue said. "That
was the alcohol talking tonight, not Daddy." Virginia knew her child
had a point, but she was not about to become a punching bag for a
drunk. Something had to change, but she didn't know what to do.
She did the only thing she felt she could do—she prayed. She prayed
for strength. She prayed for guidance. She prayed for her family.

Carrie Sue curled up on the rug in front of the fire that night.
She had once wondered how Santa came down a chimney filled with
smoke and ash. Her innocence was gone now, replaced by the realities of life. All she could think about were her parents' rings in the
fire.

When the whistle of the train blew the next morning, Carrie
Sue rose and collected the ashes into a bucket and emptied them in
the garden as usual. She took a stick and sorted through the ashes
for the rings.

She found her father's ring first, glowing red hot, then her
mother's. Carrie Sue expected the rings to be destroyed. Finding
them intact was a surprise, and it gave her hope. Perhaps it was an
omen that her parents' marriage could be salvaged as well.

She put the rings into some water to cool them down and
then she placed them into her pocket and ran down to the tracks.
The train came later on Saturdays than the other days and stopped at
the Lula Depot to take on supplies and to deliver supplies and mail.

As she walked to the tracks, she remembered something
the preacher had said the previous Sunday about how a man should
"leave his father and mother and cleave unto his wife and they shall
be one flesh" (Genesis 2:24 KJV). The preacher said that a husband

and a wife were supposed to love one another and stay married as long as they lived.

Carrie Sue didn't know much about divorce. She didn't even know anyone that was divorced. But she knew her family couldn't stay together if something didn't change.

She had an idea. It was risky, though. Carrie Sue remembered her whipping for placing a nickel on the track. Even so, she believed her idea was worth the risk. She reached into her pocket and pulled out her parents' rings and placed them on the rail, one overlapping the other.

Then she sat and waited. She watched the train as it came around the bend, headed toward Gillsville, slowly building speed. She counted the cars, fifteen plus the caboose. She waved at the man in the caboose and then ran to the tracks. The rings, which lay just a few feet off the rail, were now meshed into one. "Perfect," she thought. She placed them in her pocket and ran back home.

At home, she smelled bacon cooking and coffee brewing. Her siblings were coming back from doing their chores. She rekindled the fire and then she pitched the meshed rings back into the flickering flames.

"Breakfast is ready," yelled Virginia. To the surprise of the children, their father came in from the bedroom. He'd come home sometime early that morning. He was quiet and hungry.

Virginia asked Kyle, the oldest, to pray. He thanked God for the food but didn't venture to address God about their family problems. After the prayer there was no conversation except what was necessary. "Will you please pass the biscuits?" asked Bart. "May I have more grits?" asked Justin.

Carrie Sue was the first to finish her meal. "May I be excused?" she asked. "Just a minute," her father said. "I've got something to say. I understand I threw your mother's ring and my ring into the fire last night. That was a mistake. I shouldn't have done it.

I am sorry for what happened. Carrie Sue, do you think you could fish those rings out of the ashes for us?"

"I don't know, Daddy," she said. "I don't mind looking, but I'd really like it if you'd come help me." After they finished eating, they got up from the table and went to search through the coals Carrie Sue had poured out to the garden.

After finding none, Carrie Sue said with some guilt, "Maybe they are still in the fire." They used a shovel and bucket to remove the remaining coals. They carried the hot coals outside and poured them into an old screen. Wayne shook the screen as if he were a prospector panning for gold, which is really what he was doing. After a few shakes, he looked closer at the red glowing rings left on the screen.

"I don't believe this," he said. "These rings have melted together. How is that possible? Virginia, come out here," he yelled. "Virginia, Virginia!"

Virginia came running out of the house, taking off her apron as she ran down the steps. "Look at our rings," Wayne said. "They melted together in the fire. How is that possible?"

Virginia didn't know, but she didn't allow the moment to pass without putting a good spin on it. "I've been praying for us, Wayne. I think it's a sign from God that He wants this marriage to stay together. But you know that's not going to be possible if you don't get some help for your drinking problem."

It was a bold statement. Virginia had never been so direct, especially in front of one of her children. Ten-year-old Carrie Sue was wiser than her years. She didn't let the moment pass either. "Daddy, I think we should put these rings of fire on the mantel to remind us how important it is for you and Mother to stay together. We love you. Will you get some help for your drinking?"

The words of his wife and his daughter melted Wayne's heart. He took Carrie Sue out to his woodworking shop, and they made a small stand to mount the linking rings and placed them on the mantel over the fireplace amidst the nativity scene.

Later that morning, Wayne got in his pickup and drove into town to find the preacher. The preacher took him to the doctor, and they developed a plan to help keep Wayne sober.

It was Christmas Eve, but for Virginia and the children, Wayne's admission of his drinking problem and his desire to get help was the best Christmas gift they could have received.

That night, Carrie Sue curled up in front of the fire. She looked up at the linking rings on the mantel beside the nativity scene, and she smiled. Just as the nativity scene reminded her of God's unconditional love through his son Jesus, perhaps those linking rings would remind her parents of the kind of love they should always have for one another.

As she closed her eyes and said her prayers that Christmas Eve, this was all that Carrie Sue had on her mind. It was really all she wanted for Christmas, to be loved by her parents and for her parents to love one another. The railroad had taken a lot from their family. Now, with God's help, maybe it was giving some back through the rings of fire. On that Christmas Eve, so many years ago, Carrie Sue pondered all of this in her heart.

Advent Actions

1. Make a contribution to a battered women's shelter.

2. Make a contribution to a local chapter of Alcoholics Anonymous.

3. Build a campfire in the backyard for the family. Prepare to roast some marshmallows and serve some hot chocolate. Read the "Rings of Fire" story to the family. Use the following questions as a family discussion guide.

A. What was Carrie Sue's favorite room in the house? What job did she volunteer to do each day? What jobs need doing around your house every day? Do you volunteer for any of them?

B. What job did Nathan have? Did he like his job? Do you have jobs in your house you don't like to do? Are all jobs pleasant?

C. There was a lot of complaining in the Reynolds family. What did they complain about? Rules to follow for the next question: You must confess your own complaints. You may not tell what others complain about. Otherwise, this question may lead to arguing. What kind of complaining do you do?

D. Why did Carrie's father become so angry with her? Have you ever wasted money on something?

E. What do you think about the punishment Carrie Sue's father gave her? Did she deserve to be punished? If so, what kind of punishment did she deserve?

F. Why do you think Carrie Sue's father drank alcohol? What kind of person did he become when he drank too much?

G. Was it safe for Carrie Sue to walk and play on the railroad tracks? Have you ever played in and around places that were not safe?

F. What was Carrie Sue afraid was going to happen to her parents? What plan did she put together?

G. Did a miracle happen with the Reynolds family? Were her parents tricked? Was God at work? What really happened at the end of this story?

H. What does this story say about the power of a child?

I. What message does it have for Advent?

J. What if Wayne had not responded to God's call? What could the family have done? What options would have been available to them? Where could they have gone for help?

Prayer

God of the Christ Child,

Perhaps the best part of Advent and Christmas Day is the children. We adults need the children. We need to believe; we need to hope; we need to dream; we need to trust; we need to be surprised; we need to love; we need to be loved. Children need all of these things too, and many times, Lord, as adults we think we've outgrown them. We haven't. Children remind us we haven't. Thank You for using children to minister to us.

Thank You for coming to us as a child, vulnerable, feeding at the breast, totally dependent. You placed Yourself in the hands of simple people. Wow! The Son of God riding with Mary on a donkey (we assume), led by a brave man who later had to take his family down into Egypt—refugees for two years, before returning to Nazareth.

To think the Son of God was a child like all children who grew up, played, and learned. Thank You for children. During Advent, show each of us how to love as a child. Show us a child who needs love. Show us a child to love, who without our love and attention may be overlooked on Christmas Day. Amen.

Christmas Came After All
Christmas Day
By Janet Whittle as told to Michael Helms

Michael and I gazed through the glass counter at Griner's Jewelry looking for a ring to give to our granddaughter, Jennifer, on her thirteenth birthday. Michael, my husband of nearly 47 years, had an eye for jewelry. Through our years of marriage, he had picked out every piece of jewelry I wore.

I knew he would know just the right ring for our granddaughter when he saw it. "I think I'd like to see that one over there," he said, pointing to a simple and delicate light blue sapphire.

With the decision about our granddaughter's ring made, unbeknownst to me, an expensive opal ring caught Michael's eye. Later that day he asked me if he'd ever bought an opal for me. I reminded him that he had purchased a floating opal that I wore as a necklace.

"No, I mean a real opal," he said. "No, I don't believe you have," I replied. Even though Christmas was near, I didn't give the reason for his question much thought.

My husband was a well-respected radiologist in Moultrie, Georgia, a community of 20,000 people. He retired in 2001 and devoted himself to caring for me after I underwent major surgery with several extended stays in the hospital.

Having a physician as a husband greatly contributed to my recovery. I depended upon him for encouragement and medical advice. I trusted him implicitly. As I began to heal and recover from a near life-ending illness, Michael began to accept short-term work assignments in hospitals out of town. "People need me to work, and I need to work," he said. We agreed that semi-retirement seemed a better option for a man so gifted and passionate about his work.

Michael took short-term assignments in hospitals around the state. Neither of us liked the fact that these jobs took him out of town for a week or two at a time. He talked with his friends at Radiology Associates and negotiated a part-time position back at Colquitt Regional Medical Center, where he had worked for 25 years. He was excited about being back in his old position on a part-time basis. His work was to have begun in January of 2003, but he never got the opportunity.

On a stormy Friday night, December 13, 2002, Michael was returning home after spending the week working at the hospital in Sandersville, Georgia. He was driving near Dublin, Georgia, when his car left the road and traveled some two hundred feet before breaking apart in the woods.

The coroner suspects the accident was caused by a massive heart attack. Death likely resulted from a combination of heart failure and the violent trauma sustained from the accident. He was not found until the next morning when a hunter noticed the sun reflecting off the wrecked car deep in the woods.

Family and friends surrounded me and my two daughters, and their families over the next several days as we tried to cope with our deep grief in the midst of a season that is supposed to be filled with joy.

Following the funeral, I returned to my beautifully decorated home. Memories of our years together sang out from every room. Though all the decorations shouted, "Joy to the World," for me, Christmas was over. I wondered if Christmas could ever come again.

A few days before Christmas, my brother-in-law Al came over to my home. Looking at our tree, he asked me if I had found a Christmas gift from Michael under it. "No," I said. "Why do you ask?"

"I don't know how to tell you this," he continued, "but Darrell Griner from Griner's Jewelry called and said that Dr. Whittle had purchased a gorgeous, very expensive opal ring several weeks ago as a Christmas gift for you."

I was stunned. Al wanted me to look for the ring in the house, but I knew it wouldn't be there. Whenever Michael bought me a Christmas gift, he kept it with him until Christmas Day. Still, there might be a chance that he had broken with tradition. With my trusted friend Mary by my side, we began a frantic search.

That ring was the last thing Michael purchased for me. To have it would be another reminder of the deep love we shared. Every day we looked for the ring. I looked in every possible nook and cranny of our home, all to no avail. Christmas Day came. At least it was Christmas on the calendar, but there was little Christmas joy in my heart. Not finding the ring added grief on top of grief.

My family felt I had become obsessed with finding the ring. Maybe I had. They tried to get me to accept that it would never be found. But to have that ring, the last gift my husband ever bought for me, would at least shine a little light on the darkest Christmas of my life.

Intent on helping, my son-in-law David and his children traveled to the crash site. They took a metal detector and some rakes and worked for an entire day. They didn't find the ring. But as they were leaving, hundreds of feet from where the car had landed, David looked up.

Hanging on a tree limb was my husband's watch, an omen perhaps, as if an angel had placed it there to say, "It's not time to give up." David didn't give up. He called the insurance company and talked to our agent, Vicki. He explained to her that I was convinced the ring was still in the wrecked car. Though the car had been thoroughly searched, she got permission from her boss to phone the salvage yard in Atlanta for help.

At first, the people there didn't want to search the car but she was persistent. She placed herself in my shoes. She said if this had happened to her, she would want someone working on her behalf, trying everything possible to find that ring.

Almost two weeks after Christmas, Vicki called David and asked if he could come to Atlanta. The crushed car had been located and she had arranged for a forklift to pull it from the salvage pile.

Only a small area of the trunk had not been searched. They cut an opening in the crushed compartment and found it filled with rainwater from the storm the night of the accident. The salvage yard worker reached in and pulled out a multipurpose tool from the crushed compartment. Michael always liked to be prepared.

The man reached in again and pulled out a bag filled with water. The cardboard box inside the bag was soaked. It contained another box, a velvet jewelry box! He opened it. The inside was completely dry.

Inside was the gorgeous, one-of-a-kind opal ring, studded with diamonds! David phoned his wife Kathryn to tell her the good news. He then phoned me. He said, "Momma, I'm driving home from Atlanta, and I have your Christmas present." I said, "Honey, Christmas is over." He said, "Not for you, Momma. I'm coming home and I have your ring!" Tears welled up in my eyes. I was overcome with joy!

When David arrived in Moultrie, he hugged me and gave me the velvet box. I opened it slowly. The opal ring was stunningly beautiful. I took it out and nervously placed it on my finger. It was my "miracle gift." Christmas had come after all.

As Christmas nears again, I will have grief mixed with joy. I have moved to a smaller home that is more manageable. This will be my first Christmas in a home that has no memories of Christmas with Michael. But the nooks and crannies of my heart are filled with joyful memories of the years we shared together.

I have worked hard not to become stuck in my grief. It would be easy to do. But in working with my grief counselor, I have also learned I have to look forward to the next chapter in life. I never thought I'd face the future without Michael. I always thought I would die first.

Thoughts about Michael are never very far away. Just as the manger and the cross are constant reminders of the love our God has for us all, every time I look at the opal ring, I am reminded of my husband's love for me.

I realize that marriage isn't for an eternity, but love is forever, true love, whether it's love for a spouse or child or the love God has for each of us. As the Apostle Paul wrote: "And now these three remain: faith, hope and love. But the greatest of these is love" (1 Corinthians 13:13).

Love is what makes Christmas possible, especially a Christmas marked by grief and sadness. Love is the reason I can look forward to the next chapter in life, even though my partner isn't here to journey with me. Life on earth doesn't last forever, but true love never fades away. As I wear the miracle ring, I am reminded that as long as there is love, all is not lost and I will be able to find my way. (Janet now lives in a retirement community in Macon, Georgia.)

Advent Actions

1. Take a wristwatch and toss it to a low hanging limb on a tree. See how many times it takes you to hang the wristwatch on the limb of the tree. What's the point? If a human with some skill can't hang a watch on the limb of the tree with any ease or at all, what are the odds of that happening in a wreck—of a watch coming off a man's wrist and getting hung on the limb of a tree? It just seems like a God thing to me.

2. What small thing that you always do at Christmas would you want someone to remember you by? Why not start a Christmas tradition this year that will be symbolic of your love?

3. Have you ever grieved through the holidays? How did you cope? How should we help others cope?

Prayers

God of the Grieving,

You are the One who makes love possible even in the midst of grief. You are the One who keeps us from living in grief forever. You grant us time to weep, ache, grieve, and heal. That takes longer for some than others. This Christmas, some of us are still grieving, still weeping, still recovering from deep grief and loss of those who have been taken from us. We've found all the joy and celebrating a bit much. In fact, we've resented it at times. But Lord, You have a way of breaking into our hearts when we've least expected it. You have a way of opening us up to a special moment, a joyous and surprising longing within our hearts for a Christmas we never thought would come. Wipe away our tears, Lord. We shall not forget our grief because it's not something we can simply lay down. Yet we know we do have some responsibility and some choice in whether we choose to remain there forever. How long is too long? We don't know, Lord. But we know we might never leave it were it not for a hope in You, a hope in the Resurrection, and a hope that joy can return, both in this world and in the one to come. We look forward to both. Amen.

God of the Joyous,

You are the One who notices those who are grieving even when we are oblivious to them. We know they are all around us, but it's so easy to look beyond them. There are people who've lost their jobs, people who have lost their health, people who have lost their freedom to drive, those who live in their own homes but can't leave, and people who will never spend another Christmas with their spouse, parents, grandparents, children, or sibling.

It's Christmas. It's Your birthday! It's time to celebrate and celebrate we shall! But forgive us, Lord, for doing so without thinking of those who are doing so alone; without thinking about those who are sad, lonely, depressed, and grieving.

Before the day is over, lay on our hearts the name or names of those You want us to go to and make Christmas a bit brighter. Maybe, just maybe, after we leave, someone might say, "Christmas came after all." Make it happen, Lord. Amen.

Appendix 1
A Historical Sketch of Advent

Through the centuries, the Christian Church has developed a calendar that has helped guide the church in celebrating theology's most celebrated points. The calendar is bookended by the church's most celebrated events: the death and resurrection of Jesus, which the church calls Easter, and the birth of Jesus, which the church calls Christmas. Surrounding these two dates are seasons of preparation. The season of preparation for Easter is called Lent, and the season of preparation for Christmas is called Advent.

Everyone knows that Christmas Day is the same date, year after year, December 25. So, Advent is very predictable. It always begins with the Sunday closest to November 30 and ends on December 24. The beginning of Advent fluctuates only a few days from year to year.

You may have noticed, though, that the date for Easter jumps around every year like a Mexican jumping bean. What's that all about?

In the early church, bishops in the East and those in Rome were celebrating the Easter feast on different Sundays. Apparently there was no unanimity on the date of Jesus' resurrection. So when the bishops came together to address some deep theological matters in Nicaea in AD 325, they addressed this practical issue of insuring the same day was chosen to celebrate the Easter feast every year. Since there was no strong consensus on the original date, they felt that Sunday was the most appropriate date to celebrate the Easter feast. Changing to a uniform date did away with any future arguments about the true Easter date.[18]

The new system, determined by the phases of the moon, insured that the Easter feast would jump around within a small window of dates. Tying the dates to the moon phases insured that no one could get the dates wrong again. Such dating sounds strange to modern ears, but it made very good sense to people of the fourth century who were tied to the land. The Council of Nicaea decided that Easter would be celebrated on the Sunday following the first full moon that occurred after the spring equinox. Because of the way the lunar calendar cycles, Easter must occur between March 22 and April 25.[19]

The preparation for Easter became known as Lent. "The word *Lent* is derived from the Old English *lencten,* which means *lengthen.*"[20] It is in this period of transition from late winter to early spring that the season of Lent falls.

Originally, in the early church, Lent spanned 40 weekdays, beginning on Ash Wednesday, moving through Holy Week's Maundy Thursday and Good Friday, and concluding the Saturday before Easter. Lent became a time of preparation for those who were to be baptized, a time of concentrated study and prayer before their baptism at the Easter vigil. Those who had become believers during the year were baptized early Easter Sunday morning. As these new members were received into a living community of faith, the entire community was called to preparation. This also became a time when those who had been separated from the Church would prepare to rejoin the community.[21]

"Today, Lent is marked by a time of prayer and preparation to celebrate Easter. Since Sundays celebrate the resurrection of Jesus, the six Sundays that occur during Lent are not counted as part of the 40 days of Lent, and are referred to as the Sundays in Lent."[22]

The number 40 is connected with many biblical events, but especially with the 40 days Jesus spent in the wilderness preparing for His ministry, facing temptations that could have led Him to abandon His mission and calling. Christians today use this period for introspection, self-examination, and repentance.[23] Advent is to Christmas what Lent is to Easter. It's a time of spiritual preparation for Christmas Day.

As mentioned, the date of Christmas is the same every year. Is this because everyone agrees that December 25 is the actual date of Jesus' birth? No. Most scholars agree that this is not likely the date of Jesus' birth. What's somewhat surprising is the evolution of how this date came to be the celebrated date of Jesus' birth.

To begin with, the early church didn't even celebrate Jesus' birthday that we know of. They did celebrate His resurrection. Jesus instructed the church to celebrate His life, death, and resurrection. He never asked them to remember His birthday.

As the church grew, she began to be persecuted for celebrating any part of the life of Jesus. The book of Acts speaks of Stephen as the first Christian to be martyred for his faith. The word "martyr" means witness. In the face of persecution, many Christians chose to die (to give witness of their faith) rather than deny their Lord.[24]

Christians were tortured and died because of their faith under emperors like Nero. The Roman distaste for Christianity arose in large part from its sense that it was bad for society. The Romans tolerated people who worshiped other gods but were suspicious of the Christians who said they worshiped the "one true God."[25]

The Roman religion made room for other religions as long as the Roman gods were respected. There was a belief that bad things would happen if the gods were not respected and worshiped properly. Thus, Christians were often blamed for anything bad that took place in society because they worshiped "the one true God." Many of the customs of Christianity were misunderstood and often led to false rumors being circulated about Christians' customs and practices.[26]

The total number of Christians martyred in the early church is unknown. Although some early writers speak of "great multitudes," modern scholars tend to believe the actual number is not so great as is sometimes imagined.

Out of the 54 emperors who ruled between AD 30 and AD 311, only about a dozen went out of their way to persecute Christians.[27] Even so, this still amounts to more than a hundred years of torture and persecution and thousands of lives lost. Christians lived in a constant state of watch and had to be very careful how they chose to live out their faith.

All of this changed under the rule of Constantine. By the fourth century, the Roman Empire had started to decline, and Constantine had enough sense to know it wasn't the fault of the Christians. In fact, when Constantine looked at the faith of Christians, he saw a group of people with moral fortitude and the ability to self-organize, qualities Rome lacked. At this time, Constantine was not yet a Christian; he was not baptized until AD 337. Nevertheless, in the year AD 312, he declared Rome a Christian empire.[28]

Now, you cannot make Rome or any other place Christian by decree. However, in attempting to do so, Constantine suddenly thrust the Christian faith into the marketplace. What once had been practiced in secret was now practiced fully in the open with no threat of reprisal. In fact, this was now the religion the emperor encouraged people to practice.

Christianity found itself in the marketplace alongside pagan religions. For the first time since the days after the ascension of Christ, Christians were free to compete in the marketplace for the minds of people, free to share the gospel, even free to demand freedoms for their ideas, where before they had been persecuted for the same.

At this time, during the winter months there was the celebration of the winter Solstice, called "Yule."[29] A week-long Roman feast called Saturnalia (December 17-24) was held in honor of the Romans' own agricultural deity called Saturn. During this festival, houses were decorated with greenery and candles; presents were given to children.[30] Saturn was the ancient Roman god of agriculture and December 25 was a feast of the invincible sun called Mithra. Mithra was the ancient Persian God of light and truth, which later became known as the sun god. About thirty years before Constantine, Emperor Aurelian had officially declared December 25 as the birthday of the unconquered sun.[31]

Perhaps now you are beginning to see some connections between modern practices and those long ago by pagan religions. Before you get upset, look at this from a different perspective. As Christianity spread throughout the Roman Empire, the pagan holiday was given a Christian connotation, and many of the pagan customs like gift giving, decorating, and celebration were transformed and given Christian meanings. The decision to establish December 25 as the "official" date of Christ's birth was made by Pope Julius I in the fourth century AD, hoping to replace the pagan date.[32]

All this is a bit ironic since Christians today are so "on edge" about the secular world swallowing up so many of our Christian traditions. Christians really don't have anything to fear if we are living out our faith and incorporating the symbols and customs of our faith into our daily lives. It was proven by Constantine's edict that a society isn't changed by the mandate of an emperor. It was proven that given the opportunity, Christians can transform a society by their actions and ways of living. Whether it was by design or by accident, the early Christians used what was meant for harm and turned it into good.

Around that date, December 25, the church began to build a time of preparation for Christmas Day. Obviously, the celebration of

Advent did not begin before the church established December 25 as an official date to celebrate the birth of Jesus. Sermons dating back to the fifth century indicate that by that time, Advent had become a season of preparation for the coming of Christmas Day.[33]

The focus of Advent is to prepare our hearts for the coming of Christ. "Advent" is Latin for "coming." Our preparation should include penance, praise, preparation for a New Year, passion for truth, participation in the life and work of the church, the peace that comes from quiet prayer and meditation. It also includes the promise of God's salvation, blessing, and times of testing if we take up our cross daily and follow Him.

Advent, like Lent, began as a forty-day period of preparation, but was reduced to four weeks for the first time in the ninth century. During this time, fasting and abstinence were required. Advent as we know it today has been in place for about a thousand years. The season lasts for four weeks, the fourth being the week in which Christmas Day falls, unless Christmas Day is on Sunday.

Advent marks the beginning of the year on the Christian Calendar, which includes Christmas, Epiphany, Lent, Holy Week, Easter, Pentecost, and Ordinary Time. Ordinary Time is the time on the liturgical calendar that is outside designated seasons like Lent, Easter, Advent, Christmas, and Pentecost.

Advent is the preparation for the birth of Christ. It is the beginning of the new church year. It is a fitting place to begin, especially since that is where Matthew and Luke's gospels begin. The advent of Jesus' ministry in Mark's gospel is made possible by the preaching of John the Baptist, and John's gospel takes us from the beginning of time to the Word becoming flesh to show us that Jesus wasn't some late addition in God's plan, but He (the Word) had been with God in the beginning. At the appropriate time, "the Word became flesh and made his dwelling among us" (John 1:18).

During Advent, we not only anticipate the coming of the day that we celebrate the birthday of Jesus; we also continue to live in anticipation of Jesus' Second Coming. Meanwhile, Christians live with the assurance of the ongoing participation and coming of the Holy Spirit in our daily lives.

As we do this, we join those of the faith from long ago, people like Isaiah, who looked for the coming Messiah. Isaiah wrote: "A shoot will come up from the stump of Jesse; from his roots a Branch will bear fruit. The Spirit of the Lord will rest on him—the Spirit of wisdom and of understanding; the Spirit of counsel and of power, the Spirit of knowledge and of the fear of the Lord—and he will delight in the fear of the Lord" (Isaiah 11:1-3a). We found Him in the person of Jesus.

Advent becomes a season that focuses on the nature of Christ and the coming of all that Christ is about, all that He taught, and all that He wants us to become. Therefore, Advent teaches us where to find hope. That hope existed long before Christ came. The scriptures were about Him and pointed to Him, so Jesus explained to the men he met on the road to Emmaus after the resurrection. Perhaps He was referring to a passage like Psalms 14:5-11:

> *Blessed is he whose help is the God of Jacob, whose hope is in the Lord his God, the Maker of heaven and earth, the sea, and everything in them—the Lord, who remains faithful forever. He upholds the cause of the oppressed and gives food to the hungry. The Lord sets the prisoner free, the Lord gives sight to the blind, the Lord lifts up those who are bowed down, the Lord loves the righteous, the Lord watches over the alien and sustains the fatherless and the widow, but he frustrates the ways of the wicked. The Lord reigns forever, your God, O Zion, for all generations. Praise the Lord.*

Advent passages teach the faithful how to live while we wait for the Second Coming of the Lord, such as James 5:7-10:

> *Be patient, then, brothers, until the Lord's coming. See how the farmer waits for the land to yield its valuable crop and how patient he is for the autumn and spring rains. You too, be patient and stand firm, because the Lord's coming is near. Don't grumble against each other, brothers, or you will be judged. The Judge is standing at the door! Brothers, as an example of patience in the face of suffering, take the prophets who spoke in the name of the Lord.*

Of course, there are traditional texts used from the Gospels during Advent such as Matthew 1:18-25:

> *This is how the birth of Jesus Christ came about: His mother Mary was pledged to be married to Joseph, but before they came together, she was found to be with child through the Holy Spirit. Because Joseph her husband was a righteous man and did not want to expose her to public disgrace, he had in mind to divorce her quietly. But after he had considered this, an angel of the Lord appeared to him in a dream and said, 'Joseph son of David, do not be afraid to take Mary home as your wife, because what is conceived in her is from the Holy Spirit. She will give birth to a son, and you are to give him the name Jesus, because he will save his people from their sins.' All this took place to fulfill what the Lord had said through the prophet: 'The virgin will be with child and will give birth to a son, and they will call him Immanuel' which means, 'God with us.' When Joseph woke up, he did what the angel of the Lord had commanded him and took Mary home as his*

*wife. But he had no union with her until she gave birth
to a son. And he gave him the name Jesus.*

Such a text places Jesus in a real time, in a real place, born to
real people, though miraculously to a virgin. No story is quite like it.
Had man set out to create such a story, could such a manmade creation have yielded this kind of power? No other one ever has.

As we celebrate Advent, we are reminded that the story is
ongoing. Jesus came. He continues to come through the Holy Spirit.
He will one day physically return.

Matthew 24:36-51 is an Advent text that tells us that no one
knows the day or hour when the Son of Man will return, but it commands us to keep watch because "you do not know what day your
Lord will come" (Matthew 24:42).

These are examples of biblical texts the church studies dur-
ing Advent. There is a look to the past. There is a look to the future.
There is a look within as the Holy Spirit's work is ongoing. The con-
templative Christian does as Mary did after Jesus was born: "But
Mary treasured up all these things and pondered them in her heart"
(Luke 2:19).

If we are going to find our way through Advent, we need
to take all that is happening around us and think on it, pray about
it, and seek God's guidance and direction. We need to realize that
Christians still have a huge influence in the world. If we will begin
with our own homes and our own businesses insuring that our influence reaches to those people we come in contact with on a normal
day throughout Advent, wow, what an impact we can have!

If we don't worship Jesus during Advent and celebrate Him
in our lives, but sit around and moan and complain because of the
things we can't do in His name any more in a school or government
institution or entity, we've forgotten whose job it is to proclaim the
gospel in the first place. The edict of Constantine proved that the

world will not be made Christian by decree. It's still left up to Christians to live Christ, to be Christ to others, and to introduce others to Christ. But before we can do that, we must know Christ and worship Christ. I pray that you know Him a bit better after your journey with Him this Advent and that this book helps you find your way to Him.

Appendix 2
Living a Balanced Life

When I was in college I learned to ride a unicycle. The long narrow hallway in my dorm proved to be a perfect training ground. I could reach out with both hands, touch the wall, and steady myself. Slowly, I began to learn how to balance. Little by little, I turned loose of the wall. After weeks of struggle, I became good enough to take the one-wheeler outdoors.

The key to balance on a unicycle is that the rider has to stay in constant motion making the necessary adjustments, shifting body weight to compensate each time he or she gets out of balance. A unicycle rider is never completely still. If the rider stops moving, that is, making the adjustments, he or she falls.

Whenever life becomes out of balance, we will take a fall if we do not make necessary corrections.

Marriages get out of balance when husbands and wives do not submit to one another (Ephesians 5:21).

Families get out of balance when children do not obey their parents and when parents provoke their children to anger (Ephesians 6:4). It happens when parents do not spend enough time with their children, which communicates that their work, hobbies or friends are more important than their children.

Our bodies get out of balance when we do not eat healthy foods, get the proper amount of exercise and sleep, or learn how to manage our stress.

Our time gets out of balance when we spend too much of it front of the television, talking on our cell phone, text messaging friends, tweeting, surfing the Internet, working, golfing, hunting, or shopping. We can even spend too much time doing religious stuff. Most things are permissible, but we must learn to do most things in moderation. "Rejoice in the Lord always: and again I say, rejoice. Let your moderation be known unto all men. The Lord is at hand" (Phillippians 4:4).

Our finances get out of balance when we become too materialistic, when our wants and desires become the driving forces in our lives, when we do not save for the future.

Our time needs to be divided among family, friends, solitude, rest, worship, work, play, and prayer. It's easy to get these and other parts of our lives out of balance.

Becoming over-committed financially affects how we spend our time; it affects how generous we are to the Lord and His work; it affects our stress load, which affects our mood and also our health. The scripture says that "the love of money is a root of all kinds of evil. Some people, eager for money, have wandered from the faith and pierced themselves with many griefs" (1 Timothy 6:10).

I counsel young married couples to learn to live off one income if both husband and wife work. That way, if children come into the home and one parent wants to stay home, their lifestyle doesn't have to change, just the amount of money that's being saved. If one of them loses a job, the couple doesn't have to panic. Their budget is still set to live off one income. It does mean they have to live in a smaller house and drive a less expensive car.

Why have there been millions of home foreclosures in the past several years? Banks have been helping people live unbalanced lives. People have been living at the top of their income brackets without any thought that a rainy day might be coming. When the interest rates rose, the scales tipped and knocked them off balance financially, and look what it's done to our economy.

We are human. None of us live balanced lives all the time. However, we should all be moving and shifting in an effort to keep life in balance.

We need to listen to the warning signs. God sends them all the time. Our messengers might be our lack of energy, our irritability, jumpiness, lack of concentration, physical discomfort, abuse of food, depression, being quick to anger, abuse of alcohol, a lack of discipline with our money, a family who complains they never see us, thoughts of seeing someone else when we are already in a committed relationship, or perhaps we simply discover that we are unhappy and don't know why.

We can even be doing a lot of good things and have life out of balance. That's one of the lessons from the story of Jesus visiting in the home of Martha and Mary. Martha was busy trying to get the food cooked while Mary was sitting down at the feet of Jesus, a rare opportunity for a woman to learn from a Rabbi. Martha resented having to do all the work and finally protested. Jesus said, "Martha, Martha, you are worried and upset about many things, but only one thing is needed. Mary has chosen what is better, and it will not be taken away from her" (Luke 10:41-42).

But for those who allow life to continue out of balance, great loss will occur. Either we can ignore God's warning signs and continue to do life our way, or we can listen to God and begin to make the shifts in life necessary to bring life back in balance.

Sometimes it's very difficult for us to see our way through the forest of problems that have piled up in our lives. We may know that life is out of balance, but we may not know what to do to bring life back into balance.

There are people who can help us. Gifted counselors have skills to listen to us and help us discover where we need to make changes to bring life back into balance. That's what Jesus became for

Martha, a counselor, pointing out where her priorities were out of balance.

Once we receive good counsel, it takes work to bring life back into balance, but it's work that pays great dividends. All of us want to hear from Jesus is that out of all the choices we could have made, He's pleased we have made the better choice. When we make the better choice, life will stay in balance and we will find our way.

Scripture Reference Guide

Introduction
Luke 2:25-32
December 1
Psalm 66:1-2
1 Corinthians 1:27-29
December 2
Luke 10:27
Luke 22:26-28
Romans 10:15
December 3
Matthew 20:14-15
Ephesians 2:8-9
December 5
Joshua 2:9-13
Hebrews 11:31
James 2:25
Ruth 1:16-17
Matthew 1:6
December 6
Psalm 19:1-3
Psalm 8:3-4
Revelation 22:16
Psalm 8:3,4
Matthew 10:30
Psalm 8:3-4
December 7
John 1:10

John 1:15
John 16:28
John 10:30
John 3:16
John 1:14
1 Timothy 2:5
Hebrews 2:17-18
December 8
Luke 6:40
Philippians 4:6-7
Joshua 1:5
Matthew 28:20
John 14:25-27
1 John 1:9
Isaiah 57:2
Psalm 1:1-4, 6
Hebrews 13:8
2 Timothy 3:16-17
Psalm 85:8
Romans 8:6
Proverbs 14:30
Philippians 4:6-7
December 9
Mark 1:3b
Matthew 25:45
December 10
Revelation 19:11

Matthew 7:1-5
Luke 4:18-19
Matthew 10:16
December 11
Proverbs 22:21
Revelation 20:15
Matthew 7:21-23
Isaiah 9:6
December 12
Jonah 4:10-11
December 13
Genesis 23:24
Exodus 3:12
Exodus 20:20
Joshua 1:5
Judges 6:12
1 Samuel 10:6-7
Jeremiah 1:7-8
Amos 5:14
Haggai 1:13-14
Luke 23:47
Matthew 28:19-20
December 14
Luke 1:29
Luke 1:34
Genesis 1:2
Psalm 73:4-5, 13-14

December 15
Mark 1:13
Mark 13:2
Psalm 62:5-8
Matthew 25:13
December 16
Matthew 8:20
Matthew 6:21
December 17
Exodus 20:3
Revelation 3:19-20
Matthew 25:45
December 18
Psalm 46:8-11
John 6:15
Luke 2:19
December 19
John 3:16
John 15:13
Mark 12:29-31
December 21
2 Corinthians 11:24-28
Hebrews 4:15
Matthew 28:20
December 22
Matthew 7:13
December 23
Proverbs 22:6
December 24
Genesis 2:24
December 25
1 Corinthians 13:13

Appendix 1
John 1:18
Isaiah 11:1-3
Psalm 14:5-11
James 5:7-10
Matthew 1:18-25
Matthew 24:36-51
Matthew 24:42
Luke 2:19
Appendix 2
Ephesians 5:21
Ephesians 6:4
Phillippians 4:4
1 Timothy 6:10
Luke 10:41-42

Further Reading

"About the War on Christmas." Derkeiler.com. http://newsgroups. derkeiler.com/Archive/Alt/alt.politics/2005-12/msg00782.html.

Ann Zimmerman. "Wal-Mart Assailed on Death." The Wall Street Journal (December 2, 2008), http://online.wsj.com/article/ SB122818206309671069.html.

Anne B. Boyd. "How to Calm Yourself: Simple, Powerful Help." Care2 (September 14, 2003), http://www.care2.com/greenliving/ calm-yourself-simple-help.html.

Anne Nueberger. "A Voice of the Fourth Century: Nicholas." St Nicholas Center (2002), http://www.stnicholascenter.org/pages/ voice-from-fourth-century/.

Arroyo Sanders, Sr. "Holidays or Holy Days: Which One Do We Honor?" blogtalkradio, (2/13/2010), http://www.blogtalkradio.com/ yehowshuwaintl/blog/2010/02/13/holidays-or-holy-days-which-do-we-honor.

Benedict XVI: "Prayer Brings Peace." Zenit (November, 8, 2006),

http://www.zenit.org/article-18126?l=english.

Dennis Bratcher. "The Season of Lent." (January 7, 2010), http:// www.cresourcei.org/cylent.html.

Droke Maxwell. *The Speaker's Handbook of Humor: How to Tell, Select and Create Funny Stories for Every Occasion, Plus More than 1500 of the Author's Favorite Stories.* Harper: New York, 1956.

Wikipedia. "Easter" (October 10, 2010), http://en.wikipedia.org/wiki/Easter.

John Glenn. "Quotes Relating Science and Faith." Broadcast from the Discovery Space Shuttle (Nov. 1, 1998), http://www.ucolick.org/~romanow/quotest.htm.

"Joy to the World/Pain in the World." Perspectives. November, 1995.

Kathleen Martin. "Blended Family for the Holidays…a Recipe for Disaster?" Examiner.com (December 17, 2009), http://www.examiner.com/women-s-issues-in-denver/blended-families-at-the-holidays-a-recipe-for-disaster.

Lamar Williamson Jr. *Mark*. Louisville: John Knox Press, 1983.

Leo's Lyrics. "Boy Named Sue Lyrics," http://www.leoslyrics.com/listlyrics.php?hid=R8Q7Bb9bR6I%3D.

"Life Event Score," http://sweetchillisauce.com/Letters/Stresspic.html.

Mary Fahy. *The Tree that Survived the Winter*. New Jersey: Paulist Press, 1989.

Michael Green. *Who Is This Jesus?* Nashville: Thomas Nelson Publishers, 1990.

"Persecution in the Early Church." Religion Facts (2004),

http://www.religionfacts.com/christianity/history/persecution.htm#.

"Quotes Relating to Science and Faith." http://www.ucolick.org/~romanow/quotest.htm.

Susan Sears. *Christmas Forum: Origin of Christmas.* Christmas Past.info (2003), http://www.christmaspast.info/forums/Main01/messages/547778038.html.

The Apostles' Creed. "Presbyterian Creeds and Confessions." Presbyterian Church U.S.A., http://www.creeds.net/ancient/apostles.htm.

"The History of Advent." Catholic News Agency (October, 2010), http://www.catholicnewsagency.com/resource.php?n=952.

The Greatest Gift Ever Given. NewYorkFamilies.org (December 4, 2008), http://www.nyfrf.org/content/view/141/48/.

"Winter Solstice and the Goddess Frigga."The Goddess Gift (2002)

http://www.goddessgift.com/Pandora%27s_Box/Winter-Solstice.htm.

Endnotes

[1] Michael Green, *Who Is This Jesus?* (Nashville: Thomas Nelson Publishers, 1992) 25.

[2] Droke Maxwell, *The Speaker's Handbook of Humor: How to Tell, Select and Create Funny Stories for Every Occasion, Plus More than 1500 of the Author's Favorite Stories*, (New York: Harper, 1956) 86.

[3] Ann Zimmerman, "Wal-Mart Assailed on Death," The Wall Street Journal (December 2, 2008), http://online.wsj.com/article/SB122818206309671069.html.

[4] John Glenn, "Quotes Relating Science and Faith," Broadcast from the Discovery Space Shuttle, (Nov. 1, 1998), http://www.ucolick.org/~romanow/quotest.htm.

[5] "Quotes Relating to Science and Faith," http://www.ucolick.org/~romanow/quotest.htm.

[6] The Apostles' Creed, "Presbyterian Creeds and Confessions," Presbyterian Church U.S.A., http://www.creeds.net/ancient/apostles.htm.

[7] Benedict XVI: "Prayer Brings Peace," Zenit, (November, 8, 2006), http://www.zenit.org/article-18126?l=english.

[8] Kathleen Martin, "Blended Family for the Holidays...a Recipe for Disaster?" Examiner.com (December 17, 2009), http://www.examiner.com/women-s-issues-in-denver/blended-families-at-the-holidays-a-recipe-for-disaster.

[9] Ibid.

[10] Leo's Lyrics, "Boy Named Sue Lyrics, http://www.leoslyrics.com/listlyrics.php?hid=R8Q7Bb9bR6I%3D.

[11] "The Greatest Gift Ever Given," NewYorkFamilies.org, (December 4, 2008), http://www.nyfrf.org/content/view/141/48/

[12] "Life Event Score," http://sweetchillisauce.com/Letters/Stresspic.html.

[13] Lamar Williamson Jr., Mark (Louisville: John Knox Press, 1983) 242.

[14] Anne B. Boyd, "How to Calm Yourself: Simple, Powerful Help," Care2, (September 14, 2003), http://www.care2.com/greenliving/calm-yourself-simple-help.html.

[15] Mary Fahy, The Tree that Survived the Winter, (New Jersey: Paulist Press, 1989) 3.

[16] "Joy to the World/Pain in the World," Perspectives, (November, 1995) 24.

[17] "About the War on Christmas," Derkeiler.com, http://newsgroups.derkeiler.com/Archive/Alt/alt.politics/2005-12/msg00782.html.

[18] "Easter," Wikipedia (October 10, 2010)," http://en.wikipedia.org/wiki/Easter.

[19] "Easter, " Wikipedia.

[20] Dennis Bratcher, "The Season of Lent," (January 7, 2010), http://www.cresourcei.org/cylent.html.

[21] Ibid.

[22] Ibid.

[23] Ibid.

24 "Persecution in the Early Church," Religion Facts, (2004), http://www.religionfacts.com/christianity/history/persecution.htm#.

25 Ibid.

26 Ibid.

27 Ibid.

28 Anne Nueberger, "A Voice of the Fourth Century: Nicholas," St. Nicholas Center, (2002) http://www.stnicholascenter.org/pages/voice-from-fourth-century/.

29 "Winter Solstice and the Goddess Frigga," The Goddess Gift, (2002), http://www.goddessgift.com/Pandora%27s_Box/Winter-Solstice.htm.

30 Susan Sears, Christmas Forum: Origin of Christmas, Christmas-Past.info, (2003), http://www.christmaspast.info/forums/Main01/messages/547778038.html.

31 Arroyo Sanders, Sr., "Holidays or Holy Days: Which One Do We Honor?" blogtalkradio, (2/13/2010), http://www.blogtalkradio.com/yehowshuwaintl/blog/2010/02/13/holidays-or-holy-days-which-do-we-honor.

32 "Winter Solstice and Goddess Frigga," The Goddess Gift.

33 "The History of Advent," Catholic News Agency, (October, 2010), http://www.catholicnewsagency.com/resource.php?n=952.

Bricks for Ricks Foundation

The Bricks for Ricks Liberian Housing Foundation, Inc., founded in October 2008, supports the creation of housing for the poorest of the poor in some of the world's most impoverished countries. All royalties from this book, as well as any donations, go to the foundation.

The Bricks for Ricks Foundation is committed to helping "the least of these" of the world help themselves by equipping them with the tools and the knowledge they need to construct their own homes and churches. God willing, a BP714 Block Press will be shipped to Virginia, Liberia, and Lima, Peru in 2012, accompanied by trained teams to teach soil excavation, machine usage, and block laying techniques.

If you've traveled to some of the most impoverished parts of the world and seen the living conditions of the people, you may have been compelled to do something to help them, but you may not have known what to do. Now you know. Support our foundation.

Help us help the "lease of these." Send checks payable to Bricks for Ricks Foundation to: Jefferson First Baptist Church, 81 Institute Street, Jefferson, GA 30549. All donations will be acknowledged.

Go to www.thefaithlab.com/advent to learn more about the Bricks for Ricks Foundation and Vermeer Corporation's BP714 Block Press.

Thank you,

Dr. Michael Helms, President
Bricks for Ricks Liberian Housing Foundation, Inc.

CPSIA information can be obtained at www.ICGtesting.com
Printed in the USA
LVOW091721261011

252012LV00003B/2/P